ROUTLEDGE LIBRARY EDITIONS:
PRISON AND PRISONERS

I0124821

Volume 18

LAG'S LEXICON

LAG'S LEXICON

A Comprehensive Dictionary and Encyclopædia of the English Prison of To-day

Edited by
PAUL TEMPEST

Routledge
Taylor & Francis Group

LONDON AND NEW YORK

First published in 1950 by Routledge & Kegan Paul Ltd

This edition first published in 2024
by Routledge
4 Park Square, Milton Park, Abingdon, Oxon OX14 4RN

and by Routledge
605 Third Avenue, New York, NY 10158

*Routledge is an imprint of the Taylor & Francis Group, an
informa business*

British Library Cataloguing in Publication Data
A catalogue record for this book is available from the British
Library

ISBN: 978-1-032-55549-2 (Set)
ISBN: 978-1-032-57460-8 (Volume 18) (hbk)
ISBN: 978-1-032-57473-8 (Volume 18) (pbk)
ISBN: 978-1-003-43951-6 (Volume 18) (ebk)

DOI: 10.4324/9781003439516

Publisher's Note
The publisher has gone to great lengths to ensure the quality
of this reprint but points out that some imperfections in the
original copies may be apparent.

Disclaimer
The publisher has made every effort to trace copyright
holders and would welcome correspondence from those they
have been unable to trace.

LAG'S
LEXICON

A COMPREHENSIVE
DICTIONARY AND ENCYCLOPÆDIA
OF THE ENGLISH PRISON
OF TO-DAY

COMPILED BY
PAUL TEMPEST

ROUTLEDGE & KEGAN PAUL LTD
Broadway House, Carter Lane
London

First published 1950

To P. H. A.

PRINTED AND BOUND IN GREAT BRITAIN BY
WILLIAM CLOWES AND SONS, LIMITED, LONDON AND BECCLES

PREFACE

THIS *Lag's Lexicon* was compiled for a variety of reasons, with the object of entertainment, amusement, or enlightenment. Its apparent uses are manifold, whether looked on as a bedside book to be dipped into or as a reliable reference book.

The amateur authority on slang should derive pleasure in picking it to pieces and finding words which, according to his belief, have an entirely different meaning.

The writer of those crime stories which concern prison life—unless he has had some personal 'inside' experience—can be confident of the accuracy of the Lexicon. He need never be guilty of referring to a prison officer or 'screw' as a warder, a 'Peter' as a cell, or 'twirls' as skeleton keys and so on.

Furthermore, no previous age in our island history has offered such unique opportunities for the ordinary peaceful citizen to find himself suddenly thrust behind the barred gates of the prison block. Forewarned is forearmed.

To-day, with the biggest crime wave we have ever known and a new Criminal Justice Act already in force, the national conscience is slowly awakening to the importance of prisons and the punishment of the wrongdoer as a social problem which can no longer be ignored.

To the sincere and conscientious prison visitor and lecturer I hope this encyclopædia will provide the answer to some of those questions which must inevitably come to his mind and which he cannot, for ethical reasons, put to the men for whom he gives up so much of his spare time.

In trying to describe the English prison—I have not touched on the Scots prisons, which come under a separate administration—it is almost impossible to generalise, but I have tried to be utterly impartial.

All prisons are run by Standing Orders—the 'K.R.'s' of the prison service—and it is the individual interpretation of these by the Governor which goes to make a 'bastard' or a 'cushy' nick. The antiquated catacombs of vice and corruption—a fair description of the big London and provincial prisons and of not a few of the smaller 'locals'—are, unfortunately, still too prevalent. The open-camp prison, fortuitous answer to the problem of overcrowding, is undoubtedly the forerunner of the prison of the future. There are, however, a number of the old prisons run to-day by men with foresight and with genuine ideals. It is these men and their interpretation of the rules who make 'heaven' out of hell, and on their guidance depends the future of hundreds of men, both young and old, who to-day fill our prisons. The material they mould is fragile and failures there must be. Success comes quietly and remains unpraised and unsung, but each success means, not only the inner knowledge that something worthwhile has been achieved, but that society is better off by the addition of another good citizen.

The old hard, brutal way has had a long run. Statistics alone show it to be a dismal failure. If a man will not respond to a new system of trust and faith, then he is such a poor specimen that society is better off without him.

It was inevitable, during a five-year sentence for manslaughter, that I should absorb the atmosphere of such an unnatural life and learn to understand, if not to speak, the language of that isolated world.

Stepping through the dreary gates back into a more

rational existence, the habits, customs, and speech of prison fall away and the strange mixture of feelings which surge through one during the first days of regained freedom give way to a normal and healthy enjoyment of life. Unpleasant times are easily forgotten; it is always the good things that one remembers. Consequently I have compiled—much to my own amusement —what I hope is a comprehensive and up-to-date encyclopædia of prison slang, phrases, and terms. The potential value of such a work I have already outlined.

It may appear that a great deal of everyday slang is missing from this book, while other quite common words have been selected. To overcome the difficulty in choosing which words to include and which to leave out, a very simple formula has been followed. Only those words and phrases which are in constant use to-day, and which I have actually heard during my enforced sojourn within the walls of six different prisons, have been included. There are a few exceptions which are included only when they have a direct bearing on prison life or when they help to clarify the prison, as distinct from the 'outside', meaning.

Slang naturally changes with the times. Words are constantly slipping into disuse and new ones replacing them. For example, it is interesting to note that the word 'spiv', popularised by the press and immortalised by Hansard, without which no prison conversation was once complete, is now hardly ever heard within prison walls.

As an indication of the present popularity of a word the following simple table will serve as a reasonably accurate guide:

(M)—Medium usage.
(R)—Occasionally or rarely used.
(O)—Obsolete. Once in a while used by older men.

vii

Where no indication is given it is to be assumed that the word or phrase occurs in everyday prison conversation or otherwise it is of such a character that the foregoing does not apply.

PAUL TEMPEST.

July 1949.

A

A.A. licence. Type of licence or 'ticket of leave' given to a convict who is excused from reporting to the police. See *licence; ticket.*

ablutions. Washing facilities are provided in cells. In a corner of each cell, generally behind the door, is a triangular wooden washstand with enamelware wash basin, water jug, shaving mug, soap dish, and chamber pot (with or without a lid and with or without a handle). A tin to hold regulation toothpowder is also provided. Men must be washed and ready to 'slop out' (*q.v.*) by unlocking time, about 6.40 a.m. See *hot water; cell; bath-house; shaving*, etc.

abortionists. This class of prisoner ranges from the illiterate, simpleton type of person to the hundred-guineas-a-time Harley Street man. Abortionists are to be found in both ordinary and convict prisons and in women's prisons.

ackamaraka (M). 'Don't give me the old ackamaraka' = don't tell me tall yarns, don't try to bluff me. Also, *boracic.*

actor. A bluffer, a spiv. See *spiv; wide boy.*

A.G. Popular brand of cigarette paper. 'Give me an A.G.' = give me a cigarette paper. See *Rizla; baron; Findlay; snout*, etc.

alarm bell. Every workshop, office, chapel, exercise yard, etc., has an electric bell push for use in the case of emergency. In some prisons the old alarm bell hangs over the entrance gates or in some disused tower.

alcohol. The possession of alcohol by prisoners is one of the most serious prison offences. Men on remand are allowed to purchase a pint of beer to drink with meals and the Medical Officer keeps a bottle of brandy for emergencies. Such emergencies are few. Men cleaning up the officers' mess (*q.v.*) after a party sometimes obtain a little beer and home-brewed wines, etc., have been made in prison. See *home brew; beer*.

Aldington Camp. An experimental open-camp prison near Ashford, Kent. It was opened in 1947 and is a satellite of Maidstone (*q.v.*). It has excellent hut accommodation but is limited to about sixty men; about the maximum desirable number if personal contact is to be maintained between each man and those who administer the camp. See *open-camp prisons*.

'All away.' Order for all men to go to their cells. Generally shouted out at the end of the *association* (*q.v.*) period or when men return to their halls after any activity. See *inside; 'stand to your doors'*.

'All right?' Query called through the Judas by the officer checking or locking up for the night. It is, theoretically at least, his duty to make sure that every prisoner has all to which he is entitled: full water jug, adequate bedding, his full rations, etc. The equivalent of the Army 'Any complaints?' As one officer always has a large number of men to check up on, frivolous replies to his query are inadvisable.

Amami night (M). Any more or less regular time for searching prisoners, cells, or workshops. The routine daily searches are carried out in the cells and sometimes there are fixed days for 'turning over' workshops or stores. See *drybath; turnover*.

Amnesty. The amnesty has never formed part of the British system of justice. However, it is every prisoner's dream that there will be one and all rumours are eagerly listened to. Every event of national importance starts rumours of an amnesty. In many ways this is a good thing, as it gives a man something to look forward to; disappointment is shortlived, for a new rumour soon revives hope. See *Criminal Justice Act, 1948; rumours.*

amusements. For many years certain forms of permitted amusements have been allowed in prisons. Supervised 'Hobbies Hour', for example, was allowed even in Dartmoor as long ago as twenty years. They also had their own band, recruited from the inmates. Charitable institutions have long been allowed to give concerts to prisoners, but these were too frequently amateurish attempts with a distinctly religious or smug drawing-room flavour. To many men repeated renderings of 'The Holy City', 'Abide With Me', or 'Glorious Devon' and 'Drinking' (by the more dare-devil performer) have proved a worse punishment than that of being locked up alone for long hours.

Where most of the day is spent 'banged up' in a cell (see *labour hours; timetable*) and reading palls many and varied self-invented pastimes are resorted to. With a sacking needle and a ball of wax (see *mailbags*) a man can make himself a dart to throw at a mark chalked on his table. The same wax will make a set of marbles or it can be used for modelling. Pieces of string can be used for games and, popular with illiterates who are denied the pleasures of reading, cell articles can be piled up one on top of the other to make the fantastic shapes of the imagination. Slate, books, plate, and so on become turreted castles, and fork and spoon, even the chamber pot and lid, tied in a long chain, become some mysterious night express.

To-day even our worst prisons are visited by well-wishers of a high standard of artistic merit, and professional shows equal to any given 'outside' pay frequent visits.

'Applications?'

Simple recreations such as jig-saw puzzles, acrostics, etc., have been permitted for many years. Cards though, even for the innocent purpose of playing patience in a prison where all men are locked in separate cells, have long been taboo on the grounds that they encourage gambling. See *gambling*.

In a modern prison to-day all men to whom the stage system (see *stage*) no longer applies are permitted to indulge in an almost endless variety of games, amusements, and hobbies. Briefly, these may include cinema shows once a week and visits from professional and amateur concert parties and repertory companies. Games played in 'association' include darts, shove-ha'penny, Lexicon, chess, draughts, dominoes, table tennis, and so on. Cards are now permitted under the supervision of an officer, and as well as evening games of bridge or whist some prisons run a weekly whist drive.

Outdoor games include football, cricket, hockey, baseball, etc., and nearly all prisons have an annual Sports Day.

In addition to amusements men are encouraged to study and classes and correspondence courses are provided in many prisons. Hobbies are also encouraged and in some establishments men may make toys for their children. See *cards; concerts; education; hobbies*, etc.

'Applications?' Every evening the officer in charge of hall or landing goes round the cells calling through the Judas, 'Applications?' and any man may then apply for letters or visits due to him or may have his name put down to see the Governor (see *applications, Governor's*), Chaplain or Chief Officer (see *applicaions, Chief Officer's*). There is no such thing as 'Deputy Governor's Applications', although many men can never be convinced of this. They see the Deputy Governor only when he is standing-in for the Governor

4

or when he calls them up in the capacity of 'House-master' (see *housemaster*).

In prisons where men dine in 'association' the officer in charge of the dining-hall takes these applications at a fixed hour; often just after tea, when he rings his bell, calls 'Applications', and sits at his table, to which men then apply with their requests. See *applications, Governor's; applications, Chief Officer's*, etc.

applications, Chief Officer's. Certain requests, generally dealing with change of labour, are dealt with by the Chief Officer. In the 'old' prisons, steeped in their antiquated 'traditions', no prisoner would dream of speaking to the Chief Officer without first making an 'application'. In the more modern prisons this practice has fallen into disuse and, providing he uses normal respect in his manner of approach, any man may speak to the Chief Officer when he meets him in the workshops or halls. It is in little things like this that confidence is built up, and although there are still too many Chief Officers of the hard, narrow old school there are also many who freely and kindly give guidance and advice. Furthermore, it is a system which helps to break down that too wide gulf between the uniformed and non-uniformed branches of the Prison Service. See *applications, Governor's; housemaster; P.O.*, etc.

applications, Governor's. Any prisoner may apply to see the Governor and having made the proper 'applica-tion', he is called up next day, generally during or immediately after the midday meal. The 'call up' (see *call up*) is placed in line with the applicants awaiting their turn. Their positions in the line are determined by their position in the 'Applications Book' and according to this list the Governor's clerk adjusts the pile of prisoners' files. No applicant is seen unless his file is available to the Governor.

In the large prisons the 'applications' system is

5

usually unsatisfactory. The Governor still deals with too much detail; the issue of a notebook and pencil; the giving of permission to have a photograph from a man's property (see *property*). Consequently no Governor, with anything from half a dozen to half a hundred men to interview, can give any personal attention to a man's problems. Not infrequently Governors boast of the great number of 'applications' they take in a day. In the smaller and more modern prisons the conscientious governor is able to relegate small matters to his subordinates while he deals with things of greater importance, *e.g.* the welfare of a man or of his family, his personal and business problems, etc.

In the 'old days' no man was allowed within a certain distance of the Governor and when that worthy passed through hall or workshop all standing men were ordered to face the wall. By way of contrast many Governors to-day grant private interviews and chat, man to man, with prisoners in their cells, free from guards.

In the absence of the Governor 'applications' are taken by his deputy, which might be the Deputy Governor, Assistant Governor or Housemaster, Chief Officer or Principal Officer. See *call up; name and number?*

apron. The leather apron strapped over a prisoner's back before he receives the prescribed number of lashes from the cat-o'-nine-tails. There is, or was, for corporal punishment has now been abolished by the Criminal Justice Act of 1948 except in certain specific cases, an opening in this apron so that the lashes fell only on a certain part of the back. See *cat; get your back scratched; pussy*, etc.

arge. Silver (from *argent*). See *white; snow*, etc.

armed begging. Demanding money at the pistol point. A hold-up.

arms. Arms are never carried by prison officers except in exceptional circumstances. Carbines are, however, still carried by officers in charge of some outside working parties at Dartmoor. The only weapon provided is the familiar policeman's truncheon, worn, as with the policeman, in a special 'pocket' in the trousers.

Army Board. During and just after the war prisons, and particularly convict prisons, were visited regularly —about every six months and sometimes more frequently—by a board of Army officers, who interviewed selected men serving sentences passed by courts martial. See *court martial; special release.*

art. Art, including Commercial Art, is a very popular subject among prisoners. Visiting instructors to many prisons give lessons in oil and water-colour painting and in drawing and other branches of art. Lectures, illustrated by film strips, are also given on Art Appreciation, etc. Many prison halls and chapels bear paintings by former inmates and often these are of a high standard. See *education.*

Askham Grange. New women's prison run on the lines of the men's open-camp prisons. See *Prisons.*

Assistant Governor. See *housemaster.*

association. Prisoner's recreation time, when he is allowed to associate in the halls and dining-rooms for the purpose of playing games, reading, writing letters, and smoking. See *rec; amusements; newspapers; radio; snout,* etc.

Aylesbury. Convict prison for women. Has approximately 218 cells. There is a wing reserved for Borstal inmates, who number about 90. See *Prisons; women's prisons; Borstal Institutions; greentie.*

B

bacco. Tobacco. 'Has anybody got any bacco?' See *snout*.

badge. Emblem worn by leaders in some prisons, generally on the left lapel. Different badges are worn in local prisons to distinguish between 'star' prisoners (a red star sewn on the upper sleeve) ; a black patch for Borstal revokees and so on. Usually, when referring to a man's badge or band it means that he is a leader. See *stage; leader; band*, etc.

bagshop. Also called the 'canvas shop'. For many years the principal industry of all H.M. Prisons has been the production, almost entirely by hand, of mailbags for the G.P.O. Although this is a task that could be performed more satisfactorily by machine these are kept to a minimum in order not to run out of work. The obvious fact that machinery could do the job cheaper and better has been one of the principal complaints of men who have spent long hours laboriously sewing eight stitches to the inch. Often on completing their bags they are ordered to undo them and re-stitch them in order to make work. This is one of the most soul-breaking and unconstructive tasks in H.M. Prisons to-day.

Other products of the bagshop include Navy hammocks, Navy coaling sacks, door mats for Government departments, mattresses, pillows, kitbags, money bags for the Mint, weighted document bags for the Diplomatic Service, and so on. See *mailbags*, etc.

Bailey, the. The Old Bailey. See also *flowers; herbs*.

bakehouse. The prison bakery, which is either part of or adjoining the kitchen. All prison bread is made here

8

and a special oven is reserved for officers' bread which they are allowed to buy. During the rationing period for bread this was temporarily suspended. See *cob; galley*, etc.

band. Armband worn by 'redbands' and in those prisons which do not use the lapel badge for leaders. See *badge; leader; redband; red collar; stage*, etc.

band, prison. The larger prisons generally manage to find enough musicians among the inmates to form a band or orchestra, which performs at concerts and on sports days, etc. See *amusements; concerts*, etc.

banged in or **banged up.** There is a very slight difference in meaning between these expressions, which, generally speaking, mean 'locked up' or 'locked in cell'. If a man, at the end of the working day and not attending classes, is locked in his cell in the usual way he may be spoken of as being 'banged in'. If, on the other hand, a man is rude or disobedient to an officer, who takes him from work or class for the purpose of locking him in his cell (either pending a report or not), he is spoken of as having been 'banged up'. See also *report; do; chubbed; milned*, etc.

banjo. A 'cob' (prison loaf), cut in halves with something eatable between the halves to make a rather outsize sandwich.

Also, any food stolen from the cookhouse. Any 'dodgy grub'—food that has been smuggled out of the kitchen or Officers' Mess. See also *dodgy grub; snout; baron*, etc.

bar. One pound sterling. 'Half a bar' = ten shillings. See also *nicker; cow; calf; crackle*, etc.

barber. Every prison has one or two barbers chosen from among the prisoners. The prison barber usually tours the workshops and halls during labour hours.

9

Occasionally a first-class barber finds himself in prison and such a man is much sought after. The average prisoner, particularly the young one, takes great pride in his hair, and more than one inefficient barber has had a punch in the jaw for carelessness.

Nowadays there is no such thing as the 'prison crop' and providing hair is neatly trimmed and not too 'arty' no objection is taken by the authorities. See *hair-oil*, etc.

barnet. Hair. 'Git yer barnet done' = get your hair cut (rhyming slang, Barnet Fair—hair). See also *barber; crop*, etc.

baron. The popular press has given considerable publicity to this word, which will probably now die out in much the way that the word 'spiv' is falling into disuse in prison.

Briefly a baron is one who always has plenty of money and/or tobacco. Both are useful currency and tobacco is more easily disposed of. Although many men get money smuggled in to them the barons are usually slick individuals with an eye to business and anything that can be turned to pecuniary advantage is taken up by them. A few of their principal business propositions are selling 'roll-ups', changing pound notes on a commission basis, buying and selling food, clothing, new shoes, civilian soap, toothpaste, sweets, etc. Many barons are non-smokers. They traffic with tobacco in order to (*a*) make money to take out with them and to keep themselves in extra food and similar luxuries or (*b*) solely to buy extra food, chiefly sweet things, jam, butter, sugar, duff. The first-named are the dangerous ones and frequently these men employ a few 'strong-arm boys' to beat up the bad payers. Many men will go to great lengths to get a smoke, 'selling' their butter and sugar rations for weeks ahead; pledging their pay until they are inextricably in debt. It is then that the barons exert pressure. On the other hand, there are generous barons who traffic because of some inherent business urge, which gives them an outlet for their natural desires. Though these are rare they do exist and frequently such men help out the less fortunate and the weaklings who are always in debt for a few pennies.

Most Jewish prisoners traffic but they rarely resort to force, preferring to cut their losses rather than risk trouble. Their paid strong-arm men are usually non-Jewish. The Passover and other festivals give the Jews a considerable advantage over others, as they are able to sell special food such as chicken, Motza, etc., permitted them during certain periods. See *snout*, *Findlay*, etc.

baroning. Trafficking. Buying and selling prohibited articles, etc.   See above.

barrack lawyer. A lag or prisoner who thinks he knows all there is to know regarding prison rules and Standing Orders. Generally a solicitor's ex-clerk posing as a lawyer and always ready to give 'expert' advice on 'how to get a special release'. (From the Army term.)

barrow boy. Generally refers to the 'spiv' or 'wide boy' type who sells from a barrow or in the street. A barrow boy, however, is not necessarily a 'spiv'. See *spiv; wide boy; actor*.

bash, to. To hit; to punch; to beat up; to thrash.

bash up, to. To smash up one's cell in rage or in desperation. Frequently, with continued confinement, a man's nerves give way and he goes berserk in his cell, smashing everything he can lay his hands on. In the 'old days' this was much more frequent and even to-day it is punishable by the standard prison punishment of No. 1. See *restraints; P.D. No. 1 and No. 2 paddy*.

bashing, a. A beating up. One who fails to pay a baron is often given a bashing by the strong-arm boys. See also *do, to*.

baskets. A number of prisons have basket shops where baskets for various Government departments are made. See *labour*, etc.

bastard. Like the word 'tart' this has lost its original meaning. When referring to an officer it is used as an antonym for 'popular'. A popular officer, on the other hand, may be described as being 'all right'. See *prison officer; screw; twirl; bent twirl*, etc.

bat, on the (or **batter**). On the 'razzle'. A pub and/or brothel crawl. Out for a good time. Spend while the money lasts—easy come easy go. 'On the batter' can also mean 'on the trot'. A prostitute is described as being 'on the batter' when she plies her trade. See *trot; run*.

bath, discharge. The day of or the day before discharge all men are given an extra bath. Where the reception block has separate bathing facilities the bath is taken there, otherwise the man takes his chance with the routine bathing parties, slipping in when there is a vacancy. See *discharge*.

bath-house. The bathrooms where prisoners take the regulation weekly bath. Twelve baths per prison seem to be the regulation number for some 350 or more men. The bath-house usually adjoins the boiler-house and contains six cubicles leading off each side of a cement centre-path.

Each man is allowed about twenty minutes in which to bathe and change. Some prisons make it compulsory for each man to clean his bath after use, but many leave this to the bath orderly, who makes a weekly job of it. The condition of the 'tide mark' on the sixth day can be imagined.

The weekly change of underwear and the weekly issue of soap are either handed to a man in the bath-house or collected by him from the P.W.S. before bathing. See *bathing kit; soap; P.W.S.*, etc.

bath leader or **redband.** Prisoner in charge of the bath-house. This is a coveted job, particularly where clothing is issued in the bath-house. Those who can pay get the best articles and often a few specially cleaned and ironed shirts are kept back for regular customers. The leader (or in some prisons 'redband' only) is responsible for the cleanliness of the baths and alleyway, etc. He is frequently nicknamed after some popular brand of soap (such as Lifebuoy, Palmolive, Golden Glory, etc.)

bath screw. Officer detailed to be in charge of the bath-house and bathing parades.

bathing kit. Although in some prisons change of clothing is made in the bath-house, many establishments have the kits made up in the part-worn stores. Bathing parties are marched there before and after bathing, to collect clean and to return dirty clothing. Any changes can then be made at the same time.

The bathing kit comprises: shirt, vest, pants, pair of socks, handkerchief, and, in some cases, soap. Only in a few prisons are shirts numbered, but it is rare for a man to get his own clothing back from the laundry. He must take what comes. Where soap is collected at bathing time the man must save it and use what is left for his daily washing in cell. See *shirts; clothing; P.W.S.*, etc.

bathing parade. Bathing parties are made up by taking different workshops on different days. An officer, generally detailed to look after the bath-house that day, collects twelve men at a time, marches them to collect their kit, and after their baths returns them to their shops. See *bathing kit.*

13

beau (M). Girl-friend. See *tart*.

bed and breakfast. Half a crown; because in happier days this commodity could be obtained for such a sum. Also *tosheroon*.

bedboard. The board of planks used for a bed. Cross members nailed near each end and in the centre of the board raise it a few inches from the floor. A rough mattress is supplied with the bedboard, and in cases of punishment is removed. Men doing punishment in cell have to put their bedboard and bedding outside the cell on being unlocked in the morning. It may only be taken in at the official hour for 'beds down', 8 p.m. See *hammock bed*.

bed-bug. See *cimex lectularius; big game; dicks*, etc.

bedding. Bedding is part of the standard cell equipment and on taking over a cell a man should find two (or three in winter) blankets, a coarsely woven bedrug, of dull red and yellow homespun made at Wakefield, and a pillow. Extra blankets are issued only on the Medical Officer's authority, but men living in end cells, presumed to be colder, are allowed one extra blanket at all seasons.

Linen—two coarse sheets and a pillow slip—is issued on reception and changed periodically. Clean sheets are issued about once a month and pillow slips every two or three weeks. Towels are changed weekly. See *furniture; reception kit*, etc.

Bedford Prison. A small local prison with cell accommodation for about 120. See *Prisons*.

'beds down.' Officially beds may not be laid down until the 8 p.m. bell has rung. Lenient officers turn a blind eye to this rule, particularly in winter when there is nothing else for a man to do but to go to bed. Cold usually prevents comfortable reading or study. See *bell.*

beds, spring. Spring beds are standard in prison hospitals and in some prisons a number of these are available to prisoners and convicts, generally on a 'wait your turn' basis. Otherwise the standard issue is the wooden bedboard (see above) and the hammock bed which is slowly replacing it. See *hammock bed; bedding,* etc.

beer. Although alcohol (*q.v.*) is prohibited in prison, men on remand may have one pint of beer to drink with their midday meal. See *home brew.*

beggar's lagging. A three months' sentence of imprisonment. See *tramp's lagging; carpet.*

bell. The ship's bell used in the halls for signalling. Rung at meal times, labour time, association period, and bedtime, etc. In many prisons this nerve-shattering relic of barbarism, which causes agony to both prisoners and officers, has been replaced by a small hand-bell.

The bell is always rung at 8 p.m. to signal 'beds down', which, with the evening issue of cocoa, signals the end of the prisoner's day. See also *ringer; cell bell; alarm bell.*

belt and braces. The prisoner is given his choice of belt or braces. The belt is usually made of a thin strip of doubled hessian with a cheap buckle. Braces, often of the same material, have no 'give'. Belts are made illegally in the tailor's shop or the bootshop. These are usually extra wide and some, for those who can pay, have leather straps and two or more neat buckles. At intervals these articles are rounded up, though, except in the 'bad' prisons, few are actually punished for this offence.

bent. Crooked, dishonest, corrupt.

bent screw or **bent twirl**. A dishonest officer. An officer who 'fiddles'; who deals in illicit traffic. He may or may not be honest in the sense that he infringes a prison rule, but he may be honest in that he gives the 'customer' a fair return for his money. It is not uncommon for officers, working in pairs, to take money from a man and then to have him punished for trafficking. In the big prisons this is fairly common. One officer offers to change money for a man and having handed over the agreed amount of tobacco he 'tips off' his friend, who searches the man, confiscates the tobacco, and has the man punished. This provides pocket money and at the same time keeps the officer's record sheet in good trim. It is a practice which is more suited to a short-term prison than to a long-term establishment.

Most officers, however, unless they are heavy gamblers, give a fair deal. They generally work through a trusted leader (*q.v.*), who touts for clients. The client writes a letter to friend or relation, asking for money, and the officer later adds his address (usually an accommodation one). Commission for this service varies; an average is £2 for 'bringing in' £5. The odd £3 can then be exchanged for tobacco at the current prison rate, varying from one to as much as four ounces to the £. The leader takes a 'rake-off' of about half to one ounce in the pound. If he is dishonest he frequently keeps all the client's money, fobbing him off with excuses that the 'screw didn't pay up'. This inevitably leads to trouble and the downfall of both leader and officer. It is also one of the main causes of internal trouble and fighting. See *safe screw; baron; fiddle; buy; sell; trafficking; stiff; joey,* etc.

Bentham, Jeremy. The productive writer on politics and jurisprudence whose most comprehensive work, *Introduction to the Principles of Morals and Legislation,* expounds the principles which may be condensed into

'The greatest good for the greatest number'. Born in 1748, he visited Russia in 1785 and brought back his famous idea of a panopticon, or model prison, which occupied him for many years. Apart from a great interest in prisons he is credited with untiring work towards the reform of the poor law, the amplification of judicial procedure, and the recasting of the law of evidence. He died at his country house, Ford Abbey in Wiltshire, in 1814.

Bertram Mills (R). See *centre screw; ringmaster.*

B.I. Borstal Institution (*q.v.*) or Borstal inmate. A Borstal boy is referred to as a 'B.I.' See *boy.*

Bible. For the best part of a century or more a Bible has been standard equipment in every cell (see *cell*). Shortage of paper has assisted the authorities to use some discernment in the issue of this book. Many copies were printed on a paper which could, at a pinch, be used for rolling cigarettes, and any Bible (or other book) could be used for a scribbling pad, as a source of toilet paper, and as an object for sheer wanton destruction. See *religion; glory, got the.*

big game (M). Vermin. See *cimex lectularius; dicks.*

birch, the. See *corporal punishment.*

bird. Imprisonment. To do bird = to serve a prison sentence (rhyming slang, bird lime—time). See *time; lagging; first bird*, etc. Also, a girl. See *tart.*

Birdcage. A field or enclosure surrounded by a fence or bull netting, where reliable prisoners work in fields from which they could, if they so wished, escape with ease.

Part of the prison ground at Camp Hill, Isle of Wight, is known as the Birdcage.

Birmingham. (Winston Green.) Local prison for men and women. Built on the 'spokes of a wheel' system, it has cell accommodation for about 400 inmates. See *Prisons*.

black, the. See *blackie*.

black cap. The black cloth placed over the head of a Judge pronouncing sentence of death. This and the white gloves carried by the Judge for the grim ceremony are placed on the table in front of him when he takes his seat. Since the controversy over the death penalty (1948) some Judges have abandoned the black cap and use a modified version of the death sentence. See *death sentence; death watch; executions*, C.C.

Black Maria. The name of the familiar police vehicle. The name is said to derive from a negress of prodigious strength. This woman kept a boarding house for sailors in Boston and owing to her exceptional strength her services were often solicited by the police when they were unable to cope with an exceptionally difficult drunkard. It was said that Black Maria could drag any man to jail, single-handed, without the slightest difficulty. See also *follow-up wagon; heavy stuff*, etc.

blackie, the, or **the black.** Blackmail. 'Oh—so you'd put the blackie on me, would you?'

blag mob. Expression stated to refer to the *heavy mob*, men who specialise in warehouse robberies and who do not stop short at using violence. See *heavy*, etc.

blagger (R). Used very occasionally to refer to men who resort to violence, particularly when operating in superior numbers. Probably an abbreviation of 'blackguard'.

bleat (M). A Petition to the Home Secretary. 'The new geezer put in a bleat the day he arrived.' See *petition; scream;* etc.

block, cell. British prisons are built more or less on a standard pattern. Each hall or block varies from the next only in the number of cells. In the larger prisons these blocks radiate from a common centre (see *centre*) like the spokes of a wheel. The officer on the centre can thus keep an eye on each block on his floor or landing. Usually referred to by letters, *i.e.* 'A' block, 'B' block, and so on; many prisons have adopted names for their blocks or, as they frequently prefer to call them, 'halls'. Popular names are those chosen from people who have, in some form or other, distinguished themselves in prison work. The reformer Howard, prison governors of distinction, patron saints, and so on are popular. See *centre; landing; Bentham, J.*

blocks on, to put the. Tightening up of regulations against 'fiddling' or lax discipline. After a big tobacco racket has been uncovered the 'barons' and 'bent screws' go to ground. Tobacco is difficult to obtain— the blocks are on. See *fiddling; baron*, etc.

blower. Popular slang term both inside and outside prison for telephone. Originates from the old-fashioned speaking-tube through which the caller first blew to attract the attention of the person at the other end, by means of a whistle.

Prison telephones are generally out of reach of prisoners, even if not connected to a direct outside line. They are sometimes housed in boxes which can be opened only by an officer in possession of the standard cell key. In most prisons the internal telephone is automatic.

blue papers. The papers sent to the prison authorities concerning a 'lifer' who is due for discharge or for a special release within the next six months or so. Once a lifer gets his 'blue papers' he knows that he is due for release and word flies round the prison, 'So-and-so has got his blue papers.' See *special release; lifer*, etc.

bluecoat. A convict who has reached the second stage. At two and a half years he changes his grey coat for a blue one. At four and a half years he adds a grey band to the sleeves of this. See *stage; greyband; red collar*, etc.

blues, the. The bluecoat men. See *bluecoat; greys, the; Special; stage*, etc.

bluette. Thin blue materials for working smocks or overalls. See *overalls*.

B.O. This particularly unpleasant condition is prevalent among prisoners owing to a combination of diet, inadequate changes of underwear, and lack of proper bathing facilities. Visitors say that they can detect the peculiar smell of prison before they actually pass through the gates.

bogey. A plain-clothes detective. Occasionally used to refer to any policeman. See *dick; nark; Johns; slop*, etc.

boiler house. The 'stokehole' where steam is raised for the heating system, cooking, baths, etc. See also *stokehole*.

bollocking. A sound ticking off. To 'get a bollocking' is the equivalent of 'having a strip torn off'. See also *do; done*, etc.

bolt. Ordinary slide-bolt attached to the outside of the cell door. In addition to the ordinary lock this bolt is shot home last thing at night before the evening duty officer hands over to the 'night screw'. Although many prisons have no bolts they have recently been fitted in others. During the bombing of the late war it was found that some locks would fly open with vibration or blast. As a safeguard against this an order was put out that bolts were to be fitted. Two years after the end of the war at least one prison started to carry out this order.

bookbinding. Many prisons have a small bookbinding class or shop where library books can be repaired and periodicals bound. All printing for the Prison Service is done at Maidstone and part of the large printing shop is devoted to binding the numerous books which are deemed essential to the efficient running of the prisons.

Bookbinding is also a popular hobby and a number of prisons give spare-time instruction in simple book-binding.

Bookbinders generally manage to do a certain amount of 'private work', for which they are paid in tobacco or 'roll-ups'. Picture-frames, albums, and pocket-books are the chief products of this illicit activity and as most articles are later confiscated the makers are constantly accepting fresh 'orders' until someone is actually punished and, for a time, the 'blocks are on'. See *photographs; printers' shop.*

book-keeping. A popular educational class, particularly with those men who own small businesses outside. See *education.*

bookmaker. Every prison has at least one bookmaker. Often he is a 'baron' but not necessarily so. He works through touts, pays out on the 'dot' in money or tobacco, and, where horse racing is concerned, pays the official prices. Dog racing and football pools are run by him and special pool forms have actually been printed in prison. All prison football matches and sports event carry a great deal of money and tobacco. Cards (see *cards; bridge,* etc.) have long been prohibited in prison because it was thought that they would encourage gambling. A born gambler will always find something on which to risk his money. It may be anything from the number of days' bread and water likely to be awarded an unfortunate fellow-prisoner or it may be a porridge-eating contest between two rival 'gannets' (gluttons). See *gambling; snout,* etc.

Booth, a (M). A member of the Salvation Army, a fol-lower of General Booth. See *chapel; religion.*

boots. Boots are issued only to those men working on outside parties such as farm parties, labourers, gardeners, etc. All other men wear shoes. See *shoes; clogs; bootshop; polish*, etc.

bootshop. Every prison has a corner, sometimes in the bagshop or the tailors' shop, where some sort of repairs can be made to boots and shoes. Many prisons have large bootshops where prison boots and shoes are made and repaired, where officers' and police boots are made, and where members of the staff may have their family repairs attended to.

boracic. 'Don't give me the old boracic' = don't tell me tall yarns, don't try to get round me with smooth words. Also *ackamaraka*.

Borstal. Borstal Institution near Rochester, Kent, with accommodation for 329. Contrary to popular opinion this is not the original Borstal Institution. See *Borstal Institutions*.

Borstal Institutions. To-day with an unprecedented amount of crime committed by young offenders new Borstal wings and establishments are constantly being opened up and existing ones enlarged. The maximum Borstal sentence is up to three years, but a 'boy' can obtain parole very much earlier if he responds to the treatment. Briefly, the Borstal system tries to give the young offender an education on public school lines, in surroundings that are healthful to mind and body. Those who will not respond are transferred to special Borstal wings at various prisons (such as Wormwood Scrubs, Chelmsford, Kingston, etc.) where discipline is sterner. Borstal escapes constantly find space in the daily press, but many of these escapades are due solely to the unpredictable nature of the youthful offender. Frequently a 'boy' due for release will run away a day or two before the fixed date. Most of them aim for home, if they have one, and are caught within a few hours. Naturally this causes a great deal of work for local police and is a constant headache for the Borstal authorities. The average ex-Borstal boy who finds his way into prison is usually a most likeable type of man, willing and friendly but for some unknown reason unable to keep away from trouble. For a list of the principal Borstal Institutions see under *Prisons*.

bottoms. Mailbag component; the hessian or canvas square cut to form the bottom part of the large parcel-post type of mailbag. See *mailbags*, etc.

box. See *paddy*, which is also referred to as 'the box' or 'a box'.

box. Any coffin. A coffin made in the shops for a prisoner or condemned man, though these are to-day usually bought 'outside'.

box, to. Something cleverly done. Something which requires brains and/or cunning to accomplish. 'He boxed that fiddle okay' = he organised that bit of business very well. A 'fiddle', incidentally, need not need brains or cunning.

box visit. Can refer to either of two visits: (*a*) a 'closed visit' in a glass-partitioned and wired box or (*b*) in a small room with only a table between prisoner and visitor. See *visits; closed visit; Zoo trip; open visit.*

boy. Borstal boy. All 'B.I.s' are referred to as 'boys' or 'lads'. Officers whose early service period was spent in Borstal Institutions never lose the habit of calling all young men, and not a few old ones, either 'boy' or 'lad'. Many 'boys' are married men and fathers. During and after the late war this was very much the case, and an almost permanent source of amusement

23

was the sight of a 'boy' on a visit, wearing the regulation brown shorts and dangling a child or two on his bare knees.

The Borstal boy's uniform comprises a brown jacket, similar to the grey prisoner's jacket in cut but referred to as a 'sports coat', brown shorts (except for senior boys or 'stripes', as their 'leaders' are called), and stockings rolled over boot tops. See *Borstal Institutions; leader.*

Ex-Borstal boys generally chum up in prison, though the majority, according to statistics, never again come before the courts. Should the culprit in some prominent hold-up or murder be an ex-Borstal boy it is a source of pride for a man to claim acquaintance. 'So-and-so, pooh, I knew him at such-and-such a Borstal.' There is a distinct 'old-school' touch about the average 'boy'.

bracelets. (R) Handcuffs. See also *cuffs; darbies; snitcher.*

Brahma. (R) A girl (service term). See *tart.*

branks. A scold's bridle. A framework of iron made to enclose the head and having a bit to compress the tongue. An old Scottish invention.

brass. A prostitute. See *tart; half-brass; broad.*

brassed. The familiar service term for being fed up. Also, *browned-off; cheesed,* etc.

bread. See *cob; bakehouse,* etc.

'brickies'. Nickname given to the bricklaying party. Apart from the usual 'Works' party who carry out small repairs and any rebuilding, several prisons run a whole-time instructional course in bricklaying. The course usually lasts for about six months and men who qualify and who wish for it are found suitable employment on discharge. See *vocational training; education,* etc.

bride. A girl. The girl-friend. See *tart*, etc.

bridge. A number of prisons now permit card-playing under the supervision of an officer, and bridge is a popular game with a small but enthusiastic following. At Maidstone expert instruction is given to learners by a visitor who comes in voluntarily at weekends. Those men who know the game meanwhile play among themselves and the 'class' often numbers over thirty men. See *amusements*, etc.

Bristol. Local prison with cell accommodation for 209. Nearest local prison to Ley Hill (*q.v.*), from where are sent those men who infringe boundary rules, etc. See *Prisons; Ley Hill.*

Brixton. Local prison with cell accommodation for about 590 men. Aliens, etc., await deportation at Brixton and convicts for Parkhurst are frequently 'lodged' there. 'Star' convicts, on the other hand, are 'lodged' at Wormwood Scrubs. See *Prisons; lodger.*

broad. Popular Americanism for 'half-brass'. Used by those who affect Americanisms. A 'broad' is a girl or woman of easy virtue who does not take money. See *brass; half-brass; tart*, etc.

broad arrow. The familiar Government mark no longer occupies a conspicuous place on the clothing of prisoners. The broad arrow went out with the cropped hair and the ball and chain. Very occasionally, however, one comes across an aged cape or other garment still bearing the faint traces of the arrow which once branded the criminal. Such garments are a great source of amusement and, as with free men and women, the average prisoner can appreciate the age-old jokes of prison life.

Broadmoor. Well known as the criminal lunatic asylum where all convicted felons are sent who have been certified insane. Under the Criminal Justice Act of 1948 all 'asylums and places appointed under section one of the Criminal Lunacy Asylums Act of 1860, shall be called Broadmoor Institutions'. This also means that criminal lunatics will no longer be referred to as such but as 'Broadmoor patients'.

Officers employed in such institutions as Broadmoor, by virtue of this Act, now come under the National Health Service Act of 1946, providing for the grant of superannuation benefits. See also *Prisons; Borstal Institutions; certified; Hoppite*, etc.

broads. Identity cards. Any papers of identification, such as ration cards, insurance book, etc. See *cards*.

brown coat. Remand, debtor, or deportee. These wear brown suits to distinguish them from the ordinary prisoners who wear grey.

Brown suits are, however, issued to men at some open-camp prisons and Borstal Institutions issue brown coats (referred to as 'sports coats') and brown shorts. See *stage; special; greycoat; bluecoat; Borstal Institutions*, etc.

brown hatter. One who consorts with homosexuals. The active partner in such practices. See *pouff*, etc.

browned off. Familiar service term for being fed up with things in general. Also, *brassed; cheesed*, etc.

bubble. A 'squeak'. To tell tales or to give information against another. 'To put the bubble in the tube' = to tell an officer of the illegal behaviour of a fellow-prisoner. If there is 'no jet', it means that the officer refused to listen or to take action. (Rhyming slang from 'bubble and squeak'.) See *grass, to; squeak; squeal; grasser; tube; no jet; nit-nit; eye eye; don't want to know*, etc.

Buddhists. Men of all religions are found in all prisons. Buddhists, mostly seamen, have equal rights with others for free worship. See *religion*.

builder's party. The party working under the direction of the Engineer Officer (*q.v.*), attending to the fabric, repairs, and general 'works' jobs. The bricklaying party (see *brickies*) are sometimes referred to as the builders' party. See *vocational training; works party*, etc.

bun. About twice a week a bun, of the 'penny' type, is issued with the evening meal or with the dinner. This is easily disposed of in the prison market. See *buy; sell; trafficking*, etc.

bung, to. Give. 'Bung me a snout' = give me a cigarette. Can also mean a 'tip'. 'Did he bung you?' = did he give you a tip? 'I will give you some grub if you will bung me' = I will let you have some food if you will pay me. See *snout; drop*.

bunny. To talk. 'To have a bunny' = to have a 'pow wow'. See also *rabbits*.

burglary. Burglary is defined as breaking and entering a private dwelling-house between the hours of 9 p.m. and 6 a.m. At any other time or with any other building it is called housebreaking. In Scotland either offence is called housebreaking. See *screw, to; drum; gaff; rat; creep; sneakers*, etc.

burgoo (M). Australian service slang for porridge.

burn, to. To smoke. 'To have a burn' = to have a smoke. 'Bung me a burn' = give me a smoke. See *snout*.

burning. Opening a safe with oxyacetylene. A process which calls for skill and the success of which depends on blacking out all windows against the glare which would give the operation away to any passer-by. See *stripping; jelly; Peterman; stick*.

busker. One who sings in the street for a living. Also, *chant; griddle.*

butter, a. Margarine is issued in small pats at breakfast and at supper time. A 'butter' is one ration and is a unit of prison currency. It is usually worth more than, say, cheese and averages one to two 'snout'—the thinly rolled prison cigarettes. See *snout; buy; sell*, etc.

buy. To barter food for tobacco, 'roll-ups', flints, cigarette papers, etc. Food and tobacco are the two commodities over which all bartering is done. See *snout; sell; trafficking*, etc.

buzz, a. A rumour (service slang). See *rumours.*

buzz, to. To steal.

buzzed. Stolen. 'He buzzed a crombie' = he stole an overcoat. 'I bought it cheap because it had been buzzed.' See *buzzing; whizzing; screw, to.*

buzzing. Lone pocket-picking. See *whizzing; whizz gang*, etc.

C

caff. A café.

caff boys. The youths and men, the 'spivs' and 'wide boys', who hang around certain cafés and pin-table parlours. A great deal of illegal business is discussed at cafés where thieves and receivers forgather. See *actor; spiv; wide boy*, etc.

calf. Ten shillings. (Rhyming slang for 'half'. A 'cow' is one pound sterling. 'Cow and calf' is, therefore, thirty shillings.) See *bar; cow; nicker*, etc.

calioped (M). See *cased; weighed off*, etc.

call-up, Governor's. At 'applications time' a man may be called up by the Governor if there is anything of which he should be advised. For example, in a London prison a man may have received all the letters to which he is entitled and another one is sent in. He is not allowed to have it, but if there is anything in it which appears to be important to the man the Governor may 'call him up', read the letter to him, and then have it put in the man's 'property'. During and after the late war a 'Governor's call-up' was a signal for great excitement if the man called up was known to be a court-martial case. See *applications; court martial; special release*, etc.

Camp Hill. Borstal Institution with accommodation for 351 in cells and with a number of rooms suitable for dormitories. Situated near the old convict prison of Parkhurst on the Isle of Wight, this was originally a Borstal Institution. Just before the late war it was changed, as an experiment, into a 'star' convict prison and the long-term convicts, then located at Maidstone, were moved down. The unprecedented increase in juvenile delinquency made it imperative to open more Borstal Institutions and in 1946 the convicts were again moved. About half were sent to Wakefield and, with a few exceptions, the remainder went to the new open-camp prison at Tortworth, near Bristol. The name of this prison was changed to Ley Hill. See *Maidstone; Ley Hill; open-camp prisons; Prisons*.

camps, farm. Some prisons have farm camps situated out in the country, where trusted men are allowed to live and work on the land under a minimum of supervision. They usually return to the prison at weekends for the regulation bath and change of clothing. These camps are steadily increasing but are changing into independent units, the open-camp prisons where men serve nearly all their sentences. The farm camp experiment was first tried out at Wakefield and, proving highly successful, soon spread. See *Aldington; Ley Hill; open-camp prisons; Prisons*, etc.

can, the. Americanism for urinal. See *slash*.

candles. In most prison halls is a cupboard, painted red, containing a number of old-fashioned candle lamps for use in emergency. Many of the candles have assumed weird shapes with the heat of successive summers. There is a reserve of candles in a black-japanned box, labelled in faded script, and there is a box of matches handy. The key is kept in the Principal Officer's room. See *lighting*.

cane. Jemmy. Also, 'stick'.

canteen. Very few prisons actually have a canteen to which men go to make their small purchases. The usual practice on 'canteen day' or, as it is always called, 'snout day' (*q.v.*) is for the hall officers to sell tobacco and sweets at the desk situated in each hall. See also *snout*.

Canterbury. Until 1946 this small local prison was used by the Navy as a detention barracks. Recovered from the Navy, it was filled with short-term men and 'remands' who had hitherto been housed in Maidstone, which had already been established as a training centre. See *Prisons*.

canvas. Canvas and hessian are used in the making of mailbags. Coarse canvas is also used for such bagshop products as hammock beds, coaling sacks, etc. See *mailbags*.

canvas shop. See *bagshop*.

cap, prison. Headgear is not part of the official prison uniform but on Medical Officer's authority a grey 'fore and aft' cap may be issued. Young men very rarely apply for these because of the ridicule provoked.

Special headgear is provided for dirty jobs such as coaling, painting, etc., and the cookhouse men also wear headgear. The most used is a cap similar to that worn by artists in caricatures. See *clothing; reception kit*, etc.

cap, the. The black cap—a square of cloth—worn by the Judge when passing sentence of death. See *black cap*.

cape. Greatcoats are rarely issued in prisons (see *greatcoat*). In place of this garment a short grey cloth cape is the standard issue in winter and often forms part of the cell equipment. In prisons where they are in short supply they are stacked by the exit to the exercise yard and taken when required. In some prisons capes are issued only on the Medical Officer's authority. See *P.W.S.*, etc.

Cardiff. Local prison for men and women with a total cell accommodation for about 270. See *Prisons*.

cards. Playing-cards, being associated with gambling, have long been banned in prison. Prisoners have frequently been known to acquire a pack or even to make them from pieces of cardboard. Considering the fact that until recently the great majority of prisoners spent all their spare time locked in solitary cells, it is difficult to understand why cards could not have been permitted for the purpose of playing patience. Now that card-playing is allowed, under the supervision of an officer, bridge and whist are both played. See *amusements; bridge*.

cards. Unemployment and Insurance cards. 'They gave him his cards' = they sacked him. See *broads*.

carpet. Three months' imprisonment. In days gone by it was calculated that it took a man three months to make a certain kind of carpet produced in the shops. Also, *beggar's lagging; tramp's lagging*. See *time*.

carpy. To be locked in the cell at the end of the day (from *carpe diem*). See *banged up*, etc.

cartoons. Cartoons of prison life seem to run much to a pattern and show the extreme ignorance of the public towards prison matters. The broad arrows, ball and chain, close-cropped hair of the prisoner, the old-fashioned uniform of the warder and the bunch of keys, hanging from a great ring, all indicate the popular conception of prison and show it as it was thirty or more years ago. The age-old joke of the cake and the file is hard to understand in view of the fact that prisoners have never been allowed to receive parcels from outside.

carve up. A share-out. Dividing the weekly tobacco between those who have 'carved in'—taken shares in half an ounce or so. See *snout; carvie; carving china; Findlay, split;* etc.

carvie. One who 'carves in'—one who shares part of a packet of tobacco by subscribing to a common pool. 'He's my carvie' = he is my partner in this week's tobacco. Also, *carving china*.

carvie. Policeman. See *bogey; dick; slop*, etc.

carving china. Partner in a purchase of tobacco. 'So-and-so is all right; he's been my carving china (or carvie) for a long time.' This is a strong recommendation and signifies trustworthiness.

carzy. Lavatory. See *karzy*.

case. A burglary. 'I had a case (*or* did a case) last night', 'I cased a gaff' = I burgled a house. See also *villainy*.

case, to. To charge with an offence or breach of regulations. To put on 'report'. See *report, on; weighed off*, etc.

case, to. To observe or to watch carefully, *e.g.* 'The job has been well cased'. This means that a prospective place to be burgled has been carefully watched and the movement of all occupants noted. See *screw, to; drum,* etc.

case, to go. 'To go case with' = to sleep with. 'I went case with a tart at the gaff' = I slept with a woman at (my) home.

cased. Charged with an offence. See *do; done; weighed off.*

'caser.' Nickname for an officer with a reputation for 'casing' or putting people on report. A strict disciplinarian. See *bastard.*

caser. Five shillings. See *deener; tosheroon,* etc.

cat, the. The cat-o'-nine-tails. See *pussy; get your back scratched; apron,* etc.

C.C. Condemned cell, where a man under sentence of death awaits execution (or reprieve). Usually the C.C. is made up of two cells knocked into one, with a bath and w.c. leading off. A man sentenced to death is allowed three clear Sundays before he can be legally executed. During all this time he is watched by two officers (see *death watch*). He is allowed only a limited number of cigarettes. He wears a special uniform which has tapes instead of buttons, he is not allowed to shave himself, and he is obliged to sleep with both hands visible above the bedclothes. Special meals are prepared by the officer in charge of the cookhouse and are not handled by any prisoner. Frequently a man does not eat his meal and it is returned to the cookhouse. Normally the kitchen hands make short work of any extras, but this is a meal which no one is keen to touch and often a good meal goes untasted into the swill bins. See *executions; top, to,* etc.

C.C.C. The Central Criminal Court.

cease labour. The end of an official working period. This usually refers to the end of the working day. 'I'll talk to you after cease labour' = after working hours. See *labour*.

cell. The modern tendency is to keep prisoners together and to encourage communal living in huts and dormitories. However, many thousands of prisoners still live in cells, into which they are often locked for long hours. The cells of the average old prison, mostly built after the Howard Reform around 1820, are comparatively large, measuring 13 ft. by 7 ft., with a high, arched ceiling. Many cell doors bear traces of the small hatch through which prisoners were once given their meals and water, and out through which they passed their slops. This dates from the time of the Howard Reform, when the newly arrived prisoner was locked in solitary confinement for the first nine months of his sentence. His only recreation was the Bible, then part of the standard cell equipment. Having read this for nine months he was then considered ready for the Chaplain to work on.

During the daytime the cells are empty. A few may be occupied by men undergoing punishment (for separate punishment cells are used only in certain prisons) or men who have reported sick.

The windows of these old cells are high up in the wall and are divided into some twenty-eight small panes of glass set in a heavy frame. In addition to this there are stout bars in the outer wall. It is still an offence in most prisons for a man to look out of the window. To do this, in any case, he must stand on chair or table. Two of the small panels of glass are made to slide, so that a breath of fresh air can be let in in addition to that from the ventilators, which are set one below the window and one high up over the door.

The few modern prisons (such as Camp Hill, now a Borstal Institution once again) and modern blocks added to existing prisons have smaller cells measuring about 6 ft. 6 in. by 8 ft. The doors and windows are of a better design and the cells are warmer. See *flowery; Peter; furniture, cell,* etc.

cell badge (O). A badge similar to that worn by taxi-drivers and bus conductors. No longer used, it once carried the prisoner's number and was fastened to a button on the left breast of the waistcoat. Although the cell badge is as obsolete as the broad arrow, the button on the waistcoat is still quite common. In some convict prisons the prisoners still wear a number sewn to the upper part of the jacket sleeve. The cell badge was abandoned after the broad arrow and was in use about a decade ago.

cell bell. Each cell is fitted with a bell, operated in many prisons by a lever on the inside. Pressure on this lever operates an old-fashioned system of wires which sound a central gong. At the same time a metal indicator outside each cell door drops into a horizontal position. This indicator is painted with the cell number and, on hearing the gong, the hall officer has only to glance down the corridor to see which indicator has dropped. In many prisons this hand-operated lever has been adapted to ring an electric bell, though the indicator remains the same.

cell card. Each new arrival in prison is given a card on which are noted his general particulars: number, age, sentence, sometimes the charge, religion, and work party. This is kept in a wooden frame hung outside his cell door. When he changes location or prison this card always accompanies him. White cards are issued to C. of E.'s, red to R.C.'s, blue to Jews, white, with a red-ink line across the centre, to other denominations.

Any special instructions from the Governor or Chief

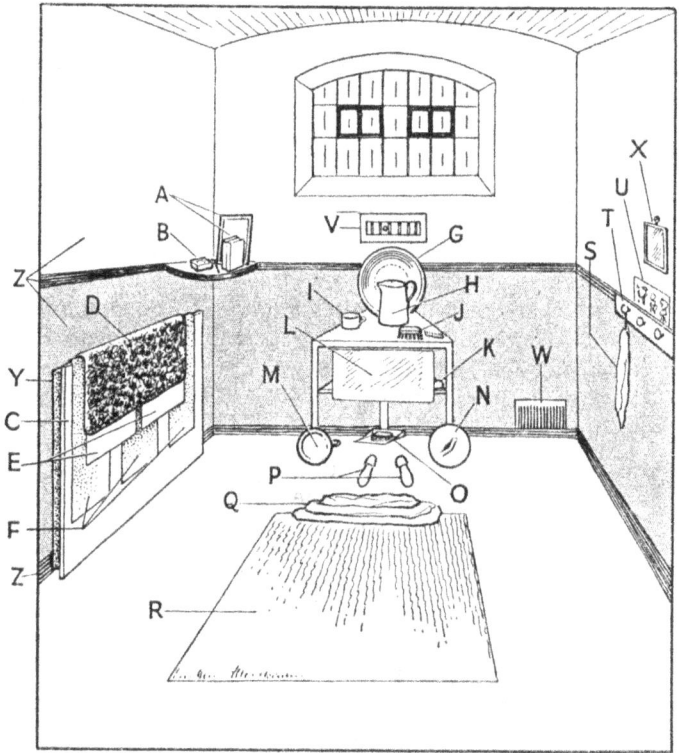

APPROVED LAY-OUT FOR CELLS

Crude diagrams, similar to the above, are displayed in most halls. New prisoners are shown these and given a brief summary of what will happen if their cells do not conform with the standard laid down by the prison.

APPROVED CELL LAY-OUT

A. Library book, slate, and pencil on shelf
B. Salt cellar (or on table fixed into wall beside door)
C. Bedboard leaned against wall
D. Bedrug
E. Sheets
F. Blankets (extra one in winter)
G. Wash-bowl
H. Water jug
I. Shaving mug
J. Brush, comb
K. Night-shirt, razor, soap dish, etc., on shelf
L. Hand towel hanging on rail
M. Chamber pot
N. *Idem*, lid
O. Dustpan and brush (latter not always issued)
P. Cell shoes (slippers)
Q. Cell task—mailbags, etc.
R. Coconut matting, cell mat
S. Plate cloth (for drying utensils)
T. Wooden studs for hanging up clothes at night
U. One to four photographs of prisoner's family are permitted
V. Ventilator (two panes in window are movable)
W. Heat grille
X. Mirror
Y. Mattress
Z. Regulation colouring: yellow paint, lower half of walls. Renewed officially every seven years. Upper half of walls and ceiling, whitewash. Renewed annually. A narrow dark-green painted band divides yellow from whitewash and at floor-level. Floors are of slate, stone, or wood.

Plate, mug, fork, spoon (and knife) are kept in the small table which is let into the brickwork of the wall beside the door.

Where a study-table is allowed it is usually placed by the coat rail against the wall

The chair usually faces the fixed table

New prisoners are shown the rough diagram of the approved lay-out and must keep their cells according to it

Officer are also written on this card and any orders from the Medical Officer. Notations may refer to privileges granted, such as having certain books in cell, late lights for study, or such things as crutches, bandages, and so on.

The date of start and finish of sentence heads the list, after the name. Also the date of the earliest possible discharge. Should a man lose remission this date is altered in red ink. All punishments are noted on the card and a man undergoing punishment in cell has a special card bearing details, pinned or pasted to the cell card board. This board once held the record card for stage marks (see *stage*). Although the mark system has been abolished for a number of years the cell card holders are still being made with the large space to hold this obsolete card.

cell shoes. Cloth slippers issued to be worn at all times when a man is in his cell. It is prohibited to wear these slippers out of the cell. Consequently there is a great deal of noise at 'slopping out' time. Men become ultra-sensitive to noise, particularly in convict prisons, and one man wearing shoes in his cell can upset a whole block by walking about.

cell task. For many years, chiefly owing to the short working day, it has been the practice to allot certain tasks to be performed in cells. This usually consisted of mailbag sewing and was a constant source of grievance among the prisoners.

With the end of the war came a wholesale cancellation of contracts, with the result that in many prisons cell tasks were discontinued. The belief, at the time, was that a much-needed reform had been brought about. The real reason was one of operational necessity. There was barely enough work to occupy every hour of the working day, which in many prisons is as short as five or six hours. See *mailbags*.

'cell task.' An esoteric joke, current in all prisons, is to refer to any pin-up girl or to any female (and, regrettably, to certain males) with such a remark as 'Blimey, I couldn't arf use 'er for a cell task.'

censor. The officer responsible for the censorship of all incoming and outgoing mail and parcels. Generally this position is held permanently by an elderly officer who is assisted by any other officer who happens to be at a loose end. Contrary to the army system of censoring letters by skimming crossways over the pages, eyes open for any banned subject, the prison system entails the laborious reading of every letter, word for word. This is probably due to the lower standard of education prevalent among many prison officers.

It is a source of discontent that certain officers have the habit of discussing prisoner's mail among themselves and, occasionally, with other prisoners. Also, *nosey*.

Central Association. Deals only with convicts—now long-term men. Such men requiring assistance are sent to the offices at Victoria, London, S.W., and may be given a pound or two, a new suit and possibly found work. The D.P.A. (*q.v.*) is a voluntary organisation, whereas the Central Association is officially sponsored. See *D.P.A. suit*.

centre, the. The centre of the prison halls. Many prisons are built on the 'wheel' system, the halls forming the spokes around a 'hub', which is the hall officer's position in a glass-fronted cubbyhole. This is referred to as the 'centre'. Frequently the Chief Officer's and Principal Officer's offices are situated here. See *Bentham, J.*

centre leader. The leader who looks after the 'centre'. He runs errands for the Chief Officer or the prison officers, cleans their offices, and supervises the cleaners who are responsible for the landings and recesses. In prisons where only a few men 'dine in' cell he is also responsible for the issue of food. Frequently his cell is a model of orderliness and is kept specially to show to visitors. See *leader; stage.*

centre screw. The officer in charge of the 'centre'. He supervises the landing officers and the smooth running of the routine.   In turn he is responsible to the Orderly Officer and the Chief Officer, to whom he hands over the 'Roll' when the day-shift goes off. From his vantage point, in a glass-sided box on the 'centre', he can look down all the wings, attend to telephone calls, bells, etc. See also *ringmaster.*

century. One hundred pounds. One hundred. Also, *ton.* See *half a century.*

certified. To be certified insane. 'He did his nut too often and got certified' = he 'went wild', smashed up his cell too often and consequently the Medical Officer certified him as insane. Prisoners thus certified usually go to the Criminal Lunatic Asylum at Broadmoor, though the name of this has been changed under the 1948 Criminal Justice Act. Now known as Broadmoor Institution, it otherwise remains the same. See *Broadmoor.*

chains. The practice of chaining prisoners no longer exists, except for the purpose of moving convicts from one prison to another.   In such an event each man is handcuffed to a long chain regardless of age or any other consideration. Although the decision rests with the Governor responsible for moving men, few care to take the risk of allowing men to travel unchained or unhandcuffed, consequently men physically incapable of walking without the aid of a stick have been chained in with the rest. The old chaining places can still be seen in some prisons. Among those who agitated against the practice of chaining men by leg chains, etc., was Bernard Shaw early in the 1920's. The chaining of men at work was common well within living memory. See *broad arrow; crop; hulks*, etc.

chant (M). To sing in the streets for money. Derives from the Latin *cantare*, to sing, from which origin also comes 'cant'. See also *busker; griddle*.

chapel. The Church of England chapel. 'Fall in for chapel': attendance at church parade (or chapel) is, in most prisons, compulsory for those men registered as belonging to any recognised religion. Many chaplains are strongly opposed to any form of compulsion and would prefer a small attendance of voluntary church-goers. Many prisons have large and attractive chapels, though in the opinion of many the cost would have served a better purpose had it been devoted to, say, sanitation. At one time there was no exemption from a church parade and consequently those prisons which could afford a separate chapel had to build it to accommodate the entire prison.

Paintings of religious subjects adorn most chapels, painted by former prisoners. Often certain concerts are permitted in chapel, particularly where there is no gymnasium or concert hall. In the smaller prisons the chapel is situated over the clerical offices or in a converted room. The R.C. chapel in small prisons is often located in two cells which have been knocked into one, or in an old condemned cell. See *R.C.; religion; church*.

chaplain. Whole-time chaplains are appointed to most prisons. There are two schools of thought as to which parson makes the best prison chaplain. One maintains that a young man should take his first living among prisoners and so grow up with the men. The other, that only an older man, with a great deal of experience, can make a success in prison. Both schools have their supporters. The first argue that an older man may be too suspicious of the men's motives; he may have been unlucky in former livings and, with increasing age, become more disillusioned and bitter. The older school argues that the young parson, with no experience of men of prison calibre, is an easy victim and will fall for any hard-luck story.

The prison chaplain's job, if he is sincere and earnest, which he very often is not, is one of the most thankless jobs in any prison. The 'slimeys', the 'toadies', and the hangers-on crawl round him, fawning for favours. Often the sincere prisoner avoids him for this reason. Only prisoners hear the real sentiments, expressed in the limited blasphemy of the English language, of the majority who profess to be the most ardent church-goers.

Struggling against these obstacles prison chaplains have done and are doing good work. Extra letters, special visits, advice and concrete help through various philanthropic bodies have comforted many a prisoner with worries about the welfare of his family, etc. The type of man who is 'scared' into religion is common in prison and it is a poignant fact that the majority of those who attend church, sing in the prison choir, attend communion, etc., are serving sentences for sexual offences, frequently against children. In one convict prison, out of a choir of ten and including the organist, nine were known to be offenders in this respect. See *Padre's hour*.

char. The familiar old service word for tea. Also, *chi*.

cheese. The cheese ration is issued once or, in easier times, twice a week. A 'cheese' is worth, in the prison market, about one 'roll-up', but it is not a popular commodity for buying, tobacco being far more valuable. See *buy; sell; snout*, etc.

cheesecake. Some prisons issue a potato 'spread' once a week with the evening meal. This is sometimes flavoured with cheese and is called 'cheesecake'.

cheesecake (R). See *steamer*.

cheesed. Familiar service term for being 'fed up'. Also, *browned off*, etc.

Chelmsford. Local prison with accommodation for 312. This prison is now a training centre on the lines of Maidstone. See *Prisons; Borstal Institutions.*

Chief. The Chief Officer, Head Warder. On this official, highest rank in the uniformed branch of the Prison Service, falls the responsibility for the smooth running of prison discipline. In any prison the 'Chief' is a very important person. Also known as *bully beef; corned beef; tapeworm; curator; screwdriver.* See *applications, Chief Officer's.*

china. A friend or companion. One's 'mate'. See *carving china; carvie.*

chip. One shilling. Half a chip = sixpence. See *sparsie; deenah; white; snow; pony.*

chipper. A prison tinder box. See *tinder.*

chiv (pronounced 'shiv'). A knife, razor. 'To chiv' = to slash with knife or razor. 'Chived' = slashed.

choked. Familiar service term for extreme disappointment. Fed up. Also, *cheesed; browned off; brassed off*, etc.

chokey (O). Once-popular word for prison or police-station lock-up, now refers to punishment cells. Probably introduced by troops or Anglo-Indians (from the Hindu). *Chambers's Dictionary* also gives tollgate as another meaning for this.

chop, to. To hang. Probably dates from the days of the executioner's axe. See *top*, *to*, the more popular word.

chopped. Hanged. 'He was chopped (*or* topped) yesterday.' The latter word is more common. See *top*, *to; executions*.

Christmas. Christmas, in some prisons, as elsewhere, is a time for over-feeding. The original meaning of Christmas, once again as in the outside world, is almost entirely forgotten. A typical Christmas menu from a 'good' prison such as Maidstone or Camp Hill is as follows (Camp Hill, 1946) :

Breakfast: Fried egg with two rashers of bacon and fried bread. Sweetened porridge and tea. The usual 'cob' and a double ration of margarine.

Dinner: Roast beef and/or mutton. Roast and/or boiled potatoes. Greens. Christmas pudding, sauce, custard. Mince-pies. Sweet tea. A packet of pressed dates or figs to each man, with a packet of ten cigarettes. Apples, nuts.

Tea or supper: Bread. Double ration of sugar and margarine. Cocoa (now replaced by tea, with cocoa at 8 p.m.). Christmas cake with marzipan and icing. Mince-pies, nuts, jam.

A week or two before Christmas the cook starts to save up rations, and few men object to being a little short here and there. The heavy eating is, on the whole, not a good thing and the wiser men eat a little and save the rest to spread out over the next day or two.

Even in the worst prisons there is always some good-hearted official who tries to make this occasion 'different'. In the 'good' prisons the efforts of the staff are surprising and when they later attend the staff party only the worst type of man objects to being locked in early. Prison concerts are popular at Christmas and there is always a film show of some sort, if not a visiting concert party. Some prisons—Wakefield, Camp Hill,

Maidstone, for example—have put on their own panto-mimes. See *diet, Prison*.

Christmas letter. An extra letter is given to all men at Christmas time. It is issued automatically about a week before Christmas Day, giving men time to write to their friends. See *letters*, etc.

The prison chaplain has a large stock of hand-written Christmas letters. These are distributed to each cell on Christmas Day. A certain type of individual writes each one by hand and decorates it with cutouts from old Christmas cards. They are, needless to say, of a very 'sticky' religious nature and all texts, of which there are many, are written in red ink. They are enclosed in good envelopes on which are printed 'A Christmas Letter for You'. Strange to say, the strict rule regarding the possession of any form or shape of envelope seems to be relaxed and the letter is actually given to the man complete with envelope. The printing can be erased, but it is more usual to stick a piece of paper over the printing. Prison porridge makes good paste and men who habitually write out 'Stiffs' (*q.v.*) frequently make use of the Christmas envelope.

chubb, to. To lock. To chubb a man in is to lock him in. 'Unchubb' = unlock. From the well-known make of lock. Also, *milned in; screw up*.

chubbed in. Locked in cell.

chucked (M). Acquitted. 'Of three men on trial two were weighed off and one got chucked' = two men were sentenced and the third was acquitted. See *weighed off*.

church. The Church of England is the recognised official religion. All other religions are allowed freedom of worship so far as possible. In every prison, even the very small ones, the opportunity for receiving the Sacrament of Holy Communion is presented every

Sunday morning. Confirmation classes are held in most prisons and are prepared by the Chaplain. See *religion; chaplain; chapel*.

Church Army. This body does a great deal of prison work. Preachers are provided to fill gaps. Evangelists and Sisters act as assistants to the chaplains and through their Prisoners' Family Aid Department many families of prisoners have been helped, particularly in the London area. See *chapel; D.P.A.*

cimex lectularius. The common bed-bug with which some prisons have long been infested. Experiments in the disinfestation of these prisons are difficult while they remain occupied. Pentonville, emptied at the beginning of the war, was specially treated and an attempt to disinfest Wandsworth by the erection of hydrocyanic gas chambers was thwarted by bombing. See *dicks; big game*.

cinema. See *amusements; concerts; films*, etc.

civilian instructor. The Prison Service employs a number of civilian instructors for, say, Engineering, Basket-making, Bricklaying, Carpentry, etc. Such posts are usually non-pensionable to newcomers, but those who entered the service before a certain date were circularised in 1948 and given the opportunity of becoming absorbed into the Civil Service. The post usually carries an emolument, with extras, in the neighbourhood of £400 p.a. See *prison officer; porter; clerical staff*, etc.

civvie. Anyone who is not a prisoner or member of the uniformed Prison Service.

cleaning materials. It is the common excuse of men accused of having dirty or untidy cells that they had 'nothing to clean it with'. To a great extent this is true. A small dustpan and brush once formed part of the cell equipment. In many prisons the brush has been with-drawn and one broom provided for some twenty to thirty cells. The time allowed between unlocking and breakfast is very short and many do not thus get near the one broom. Cleaning rags are officially prohibited, but their possession is frequently 'winked at' if a man makes a real effort to keep his cell tidy. The difficulty in obtaining such rags is the main cause of damage to shirts, etc. See *cell*.

clerical officer. Uniformed officer engaged on clerical duties. He is usually clerk to the Chief Officer and, in addition to clerical duties, may be called on for such routine jobs as the exigencies of the service demand. He is not to be confused with the clerical staff. See *clerical staff; prison officer*.

clerical staff. The clerical staff are not members of the uniformed part of the Prison Service. They work under the supervision of the Governor and the Steward, and have very little contact with the prisoners. See also above and *prison officer*.

clink (O). From the old Clink Prison in Southwark, demolished in the eighteenth century. See also *chokey*.

clock him (M). Watch him. Keep your eyes on him. See *eye eye; nit nit; case*, etc.

clogs. Wooden-soled boots used by men working under damp conditions, such as kitchen hands, fish cleaners, etc. See *boots*.

closed visit. During the first few weeks in prison visits are held in small boxes situated at the 'gate'. The prisoner and visitor face each other through a glass partition. Perforated zinc strips on either side of the glass facilitate conversation. The passing of illicit articles is thus virtually impossible but, as with most things in prisons, the difficulty has been overcome. A certain box may have a loose glass panel which can be raised just enough to permit a pound note to be slipped under when the patrolling officer has passed. To prevent articles being thrown over the top it is covered with wire netting, but it is sometimes possible, taking a great risk, to work a rolled-up letter along the top of the wire.

In some prisons 'closed visit' has a different meaning and is used for 'open visit', where a man and his friends meet in an open room, sometimes without even a table between them. Abuse of this type of visit leads to stern punishment, and after a visit a man is often given a thorough searching. See *visits; open visits; Zoo trip.*

Clothing Board. A committee of prison officials (the Governor, Padre, Chief Officer, etc.) who, with the local representative of the D.P.A., inspect all clothing belonging to men due for discharge. That which is considered unfit is disposed of and the prisoner given new articles from the D.P.A. It is a duty of the Governor to see that a man leaves prison suitably dressed. See *D.P.A.; Central Association,* etc.

coaling sacks. Sacks used for coaling H.M. ships and made in the prison bagshop or in cell as a cell task. These are made of stout canvas into which the Government broad arrow is worked with sacking thread. The eyeholes for the ropes also have to be stitched round and the work on one coaling sack is about three times that involved in the sewing of hessian mailbags. See *bagshop; cell task; mailbags.*

cob. The regulation prison 'loaf' of about 8 oz. weight. 'A cob and butter' = a prison loaf and a margarine ration. Together these commodities are worth anything from one to three 'roll-ups' in the prisoners' market. The word 'cob' is comparatively common in parts of the north of England. See *buy; sell; snout,* etc.

48

'cobitis.' Too much of any one thing, particularly food, *i.e.*, 'cob', day after day. Loss of appetite through monotony of food. See also *debtor's colic; whanker's doom*, etc.

cock and hen. Ten pounds (rhyming slang, ten—hen). Half a cock = £5. See also *flim; crackle; nicker*.

cocoa, evening. Cocoa has for long been a standard commodity in British prisons. The ship's cocoa has a high fat content and often a new prisoner thinks that his cocoa has been made in a boiler previously used for soup. The fat is often saved and used by those prisoners who occasionally get the opportunity to fry bread or potatoes.

Cocoa has always been issued (the regulation pint per man) with the evening meal (see *supper*). Numerous representations were made to the authorities concerned, to increase the food allowance to prisoners on the grounds that they had nothing at all to last from the 4.45 p.m. supper (see *supper*) to the 7 a.m. breakfast. As a concession the evening meal was changed to bread and margarine with tea, instead of with cocoa, and the cocoa is now issued at 8 p.m. in cells. The extra work has necessarily caused a certain amount of grumbling among the prison officers, but in many prisons the buckets are carried by landing cleaners who follow the officer round as he unlocks the cells. This concession was introduced early in 1948. See *diet*, etc.

coir. Coir is used for stuffing mattresses and pillows intended for the use of prisoners. Unravelling bales of this material is a dusty and unpleasant job and where it is 'teased' by claws there is usually an induced draught to carry the dust outside by means of pipe and electric fan. See *bagshop; flock*, etc.

'collar felt.' To 'get your collar felt (or touched)' is to be arrested or stopped by the police. From the police habit of touching a man on the collar, or shoulder, when it is wished to interrogate him. See *touched; done.*

colony, farm. An experiment, first tried at Wakefield, where men working on the land actually live in huts situated away from the prison. They usually return to the prison at weekends for changes of clothing, bathing, etc. This has led to the establishment of the open-camp prisons, which are proving so successful. (See *Aldington; Ley Hill.*) Borstal boys have long been permitted to work in healthful surroundings and the extension of the system to prisoners was first tried with farm parties (*q.v.*), who, after the day's work, return to their prisons for the night. Shortage of labour during the war encouraged the Prison Commission to make further experiments in this direction. See *open-camp prisons.*

common fund. Every prisoner earning money subscribes to a common fund which is spent on such things as prizes for Sports Day, concerts, etc. The contribution is one halfpenny for men earning less than sixpence a day and one penny for those earning more than that amount. See *pay.*

con, a. A convict (*q.v.*). 'Ex-con' = ex-convict or one who has served a sentence of penal servitude. A convict is not necessarily an 'old lag' (*q.v.*). To qualify for this dubious title a man must first serve several sentences of penal servitude, by which time he is classed as an habitual criminal or recidivist (*q.v.*). See *lagging; penal servitude.*

con man. A professional confidence trickster. See *con, to.*

con stakes (M). A potential victim of the confidence trick is spoken of as 'being in the con stakes'. In such cases everyone can see what is going to happen except the victim himself. See *con, to.*

50

con, to. To work the confidence trick. To cheat anyone out of his possessions by first working up confidence or friendship with him. A favourite trick of the small-time 'con man' is to cash worthless cheques ('stumers'). Passing such cheques is, however, not a felony and is classed as a misdemeanour. See *gessump*.

concerts. Amateur and professional companies are both generous in their offers to perform at numerous prisons. Some shows are of a high standard. Most are given with sincere generosity, but there is occasionally some-one who is out for self-advertisement. In many of the small local prisons the standard of concerts is low, being mostly good-hearted attempts by the local 'glee club', etc. Where a gymnasium or concert hall is not available the prison chapel or a workshop is used for the occasion. Many prisons organise their own concerts, plays, pantomimes, etc. See *amusements*.

contraband. See *trafficking*.

convict. As distinct from an ordinary prisoner a convict was one serving a sentence of penal servitude, the mini-mum sentence of which was three years. Term now ob-solete. See *P.S.; con, a; Criminal Justice Act; time.*

convictitis. One of several 'prison diseases'. A prison officer after many years of service is spoken of as suffering from 'convictitis' when his nerve goes and he begins to imagine that every convict he sees is about to attack him. See *cobitis; debtor's colic; whanker's doom; gate fever.*

cop. Policeman. There are various theories as to the origin of this well-known word. That 'bobby' comes from Sir Robert Peel, whose Act of 1829 established the London Metropolitan Police, is a well-known fact. It may derive from 'copper', which is said to come from the large copper buttons worn by Peel's police. Some suggest that it means 'constabularies of police' or that it is an adaptation of 'to cop', to catch.

cop, to. To get something for nothing. To be given a tip for doing some small service. A prisoner does some small job for an officer who, as a reward, gives him a cigarette or two. The man is said to have 'copped'.

Also, if a man succeeds in taking money or tobacco while on a visit, he also has 'copped'. If he is caught he is spoken of as having been 'done'. See *fiddling*, etc.

copped a packet. Given a sentence of preventive detention. See *P.D.; recidivist.*

copper. Familiar old word for policeman (from rhyming slang, grasshopper—copper). See *cop* (above); *grasser; flattie; bogie; slop; dick,* etc.

corned beef or **bully beef.** Popular term for the Chief Officer (rhyming slang, chief—beef). Also, *tapeworm; curator,* etc.

corned beef. Also rhyming slang for 'thief'. See *tea-leaf.*

corporal punishment. The Criminal Justice Act of 1948 (*q.v.*) abolishes corporal punishment in any prison or similar institution except for mutiny, incitement to mutiny, or gross personal violence against an officer. Such punishment, however, may be ordered only by a Visiting Committee (*q.v.*) and may not exceed 18 strokes of the 'cat' or birch for a male over eighteen years of age and 12 strokes, of the birch only, for one under that age. Additional punishment, solitary confinement, bread and water, etc., may not be ordered if sentence of flogging is carried out. See *punishments; P.D. No.* 1 *and No.* 2.

correspondence courses. Correspondence courses in a number of subjects are available, free, to most prisoners. See *education.*

'costyer.' 'It will cost you something.' Among the most popular expressions, this means that if you make a request for a certain commodity you can have it

providing you can pay. 'Can you get me some sugar?'
'Yes, but it'll "costyer"' = you can have the sugar,
but you will have to pay well for it. It is extensively
used in a jocular manner between friends. See also
drop; bung, to; cop, to.

court martial. Men sentenced to penal servitude or
imprisonment by courts martial usually serve their
time in the civil prisons. They are, however, the responsibility of the service to which they belong. Many men
serving sentences passed in the civil courts have, or
had, court martials awaiting them on discharge (see
escort). During and immediately after the war the percentage of these was naturally high. Sentences passed
by courts martial were constantly under review and it
was an almost daily occurrence for court-martial men
to be 'called up' before the Governor to hear of reduc-
tions in their sentences or that a 'special release' (*q.v.*)
had come through. This caused a great deal of discontent
among civil prisoners, whose cases are rarely, if ever,
reviewed to the extent that a substantial reduction of
sentence is given. Furthermore, men granted such
special releases, if they had been troublesome prisoners,
were not affected by loss of remission awarded by the
Governor or Visiting Committee (*q.v.*). Loss of remission, far more than fear of dietary punishment (see
P.D. No. 1), is a greater deterrent to the would-be
wayward prisoner. See *Army Board.*

cow. One pound sterling. 'Cow and calf' = thirty
shillings (rhyming slang, calf—half). See *calf; nicker,*
etc.

cozzer (M). Detective or police constable. See *bogey;
dick; slop; flattie; copper; nark,* etc.

cozzy (M). Men's lavatory. See *karzie.*

crackle. Bank-notes. Five pounds and upwards. See
flim, etc.

53

crash down (M). To sleep; to have a nap; to go to bed. Used more by tramps. See *kip; doss*.

creep, to. A system of robbery adopted by some prostitutes. Working in pairs—or perhaps a pimp will work with a prostitute—the one entertains the 'client' while the other goes through his pockets. An attempt is always made to persuade the victim to undress in another room.

creeper. A burglar; a cat burglar. Contrary to common belief the burglar never walks on his toes. Wearing only socks, or rubber shoes ('creepers' or 'sneakers'), he walks on the outsides of his feet, as there is less danger of noise from loose boards, etc., by distributing the weight more evenly. See *screwsman; drum*.

creeping. Housebreaking or entering. In one door and out of another for a quick look round, picking up anything of value on the way. This small-time class of crime is usually carried out while the male members of the house are out at work and their womenfolk are occupied in garden or yard. See *case; snow-dropping*.

Criminal Justice Act, 1948. This long-awaited Act is now in process of being applied to the English prison of to-day. In anticipation of this reform a certain amount has already been done, but a great deal remains and it must necessarily be several years before every clause is actually in effect. Though perhaps not so comprehensive as the original Bill introduced by Lord Templewood in 1939—a Bill shelved by the outbreak of war—it should do much to help the young offender and to protect society against the habitual criminal.

Where the prison system has already been altered or is about to be altered because of this Act, this 'Lexicon' has been amended accordingly. Possible changes, which may take years to bring about, have been ignored and the system described is the one in force to-day and which is unlikely to be subject to any sudden change.

It would be impossible, in the limited space available, to give an adequate summary of the entire Act, but the three most important considerations are set out by the Commissioners in their report for 1945. So far as the prison system is concerned these are:

(1) The abolition of sentences of penal servitude and imprisonment with hard labour, and of the triple division of offenders.

(2) The eventual prohibition of imprisonment for persons under 21 years of age, and the provision of alternative methods of treatment.

(3) The provision for persistent offenders of certain forms of detention in substitution for the present sentence of preventive detention.

In addition to the above the official preamble to the Act (11 & 12 Geo. 5, Criminal Justice Act, 1948, Ch. 58) adds: 'abolish . . . whipping; to amend the law relating to the probation of offenders and otherwise to reform existing methods and provide new methods of dealing with offenders and persons liable to imprisonment; to amend the laws relating to the proceedings of criminal courts, including the law relating to evidence before such courts; to abolish privilege of peerage in criminal proceedings; to regulate the management of prisons and other institutions and the treatment of offenders', etc. (30 July 1948). See *divisions; hard labour; Y.P.; recidivist*, etc.

C.R.O. Criminal Records Office. On discharge all convicts are photographed and their thumb- and finger-prints recorded on a special form. They sign this and it is sent to Scotland Yard for record purposes. See *dabs; darbies; licence*, etc.

crop, prison. The shaved head or prison crop of caricature is a thing of the past. A man's head may only be cropped or shaved by order of the Medical Officer, on health grounds, or by Governor's permission if a man should have the whim for such a haircut. See *haircut; barber; barnet.*

cuffs. Handcuffs. 'Cuffed and chained' = handcuffed in pairs to a long chain, the still current system of moving men from one place to another unless they are 'star' prisoners travelling by motor coach. See *bracelets; darbies; snitcher.*

cushy. Easy. Familiar old word which distinguishes an 'easy' prison from a 'bastard nick'.

cut, the. Any district where goods are bought and sold with a minimum of questions asked. Petticoat Lane, for example. Probably from 'short cut' or 'short way', a back alley or street. See *manor.*

D

'D' (one D). One penny. See *deener; chip; sparsie,* etc.

dabs. Finger-prints. 'Mug and dabs' = photo and fingerprints for criminal records.

darbies. Finger-prints (see above). Also, handcuffs. See *restraints; bracelets; snitcher.*

darry. Look. 'Let's have a darry at your reader' = let me have a look at your book.

Dartmoor. Convict prison with cell accommodation for 800. Men sent to Dartmoor to-day are usually of the 'tough' type. The system is designed to modify this. Trouble-makers and men who do not co-operate in the more up-to-date prisons usually finish up in Dartmoor.

Although it was once closed, as being antiquated and insanitary, it was necessary to reopen it, first as a detention barracks for the Army and then again as a convict prison, which it had been since the days of the Napoleonic Wars. Dartmoor convicts have a unique privilege, granted by Queen Victoria; they are the only prisoners allowed to keep mice as pets. In every prison are a few 'old Dartmoor screws'. These officers like to speak of the Dartmoor they knew when they were young; when the underpaid warders carried sabres and they wielded considerable power over the lives of the convicts. Many of these warders admit that the mutiny, which created so much publicity, was inevitable and express sympathetic views towards the prisoners who were driven to such drastic lengths. Recently one wing has been reserved as a Borstal Institution for certain types of Borstal 'boys'. See *Prisons; Borstal Institutions*, etc.

death sentence. The jury, having found a man guilty of murder, do so with the full knowledge that there is only one sentence that can be passed on the convicted man. That is the death sentence, over which there has been so much controversy since the introduction of the Criminal Justice Act of 1948. In order to pass this Act into law it was decided to delete the clause relating to the abolition of the death penalty.

Up to the introduction of the Act it had been the practice for the Judge to place the black cap on his head, while wearing the white gloves. Sentence was then pronounced as follows (according to Halsbury's *Laws of England*): 'The sentence of the court upon you is that you be taken from this place to a lawful prison and thence to a place of execution and that you be there hanged by the neck until you be dead; and that your body be afterwards buried within the precincts of the prison in which you shall have been confined before your execution. And may the Lord have mercy on your soul.' Sentence having been passed, the Chaplain was called on to rise and say 'Amen'. The Judge then addressed the jury: 'Having served on this jury, all members are exempt from further jury service for a period of ten years.'

The first death sentence passed since the decision to defer discussion on the abolition of the death penalty, was made by Mr. Justice Hilbery in April 1948. Passing sentence on the murderer of P.C. Edgar at Winchmore Hill in February, Mr. Justice Hilbery used a modified form of sentence which it was thought would remain in use until the question of capital punishment had been settled. In this case, the black cap (*q.v.*) and white gloves lying on the desk before him, the Judge passed sentence thus: 'The sentence of the court on you is the sentence prescribed by the law, namely, that you will suffer death by hanging.' The Chaplain was not called on to say the usual 'Amen'. However, in 1949, by which time numerous sentences of death had been passed, the old sentence and the black cap came into use again. See *executions; C.C.; H.M.P.; topped; chopped; death watch; hangman; lime*, etc.

death sentence, U.S.A. The sentence of death passed in the U.S.A. is as brief as our modified formula and runs: 'I sentence you to be committed to a felon's cell and there to be safely kept until the —— day of —— in the year of Our Lord ——, at which time you shall suffer death by electrocution: and may God have mercy on your soul.' See *executions*, etc.

death watch. The officers detailed to stay with a condemned man. These officers are drawn from prisons all over the country, two from each. There is a standing duty roster for 'C.C. duty' (*q.v.*), and officers are liable to be called on whenever sentence of death is passed. All the time he is in the condemned cell two officers are with the doomed man and two more are on call as reliefs. For this reason the death watch is occasionally referred to as the 'queer quartet'.

Officers who have done this duty frequently react in unexpected ways. To many it is something to be looked forward to. Often the mildest, quiet type of officer likes this work. The 'tough', hard-bitten old-time warder prefers to avoid it. To the few it is a sad duty and, no matter for what heinous crime the man is hanged, it often leaves a depressing effect on the death watch. Officers returning from this duty are given leave. See *executions*, etc.

debtor's colic. Any feigned illness whereby a man can get into hospital, or remain sick in his cell (see *R.I.C.*) in order to avoid meeting his creditors. Every prison has its bad payers and when these report sick word goes round that 'so-and-so has debtor's colic'. See *gate fever; cobitis; convictitis*, etc.

deener. One penny. In Australian slang, one shilling. See *D*.

dentists. The prison dentist is a local dentist who pays periodical visits. His methods are not the most up-to-date but his services are free and will, no doubt, continue to be so under the new Health Act, which makes dentures, etc., available to all. The prison Medical Officer frequently pulls teeth. See *hospital; M.O.*

dep. The Deputy Governor of a prison. See *screwdriver*, etc.

deport, a. One awaiting deportation. These are usually located at Brixton and wear brown uniforms (or their own clothes). See *remand; lay about; brown coat*, etc.

deportation. The practice of deporting convicts ceased many years ago, though the term penal servitude has only recently been abolished by the Criminal Justice Act of 1948. Records in most old convict prisons show vicious sentences for the most trivial offences. At Parkhurst, for example, women and boys were once kept awaiting a convict ship. Sentences passed on mere children were of seven and ten years for stealing nothing more than a loaf of bread. See *P.S.*

depth-charge. Prison 'duff' (see *duff*). Anything heavy or stodgy, such as dumplings.

deserter. See *trotter; trot, on the; on the run; on the batter; court martial; filter.*

detention. Service detention barracks. Short court-martial sentences are spent in detention, the longer sentences being served in ordinary prisons. See *court martial; digger, the.*

devil (R). A 'redband' is sometimes called a 'devil', dating from the days of the *redcollar* (*q.v.*).

dhobying. All washing is done in the prison laundry and, for those who can pay, men working in the laundry will supply clean shirts, often starched and bleached, carefully washed and creased trousers, clean socks and underwear, etc. (see *P.W.S.*). There are, however, a few prisoners with opportunities for private dhobying who wash their own spare shirt and socks and dry them as best they can. Officially this is against the rules, but if a man is unobtrusive, he can usually 'get away with it'. See *laundry.*

diabetics. Diabetics are allowed special diet and are frequently given jobs in the prison hospital. See *diet; hospital*, etc.

dick. Detective. See *bogey; nark; copper*, etc.

dicks. Lice. Vermin. See *Cimex lectularius; big game*, etc. (It will be noted that detectives and vermin are referred to by the same word.)

didikai. Non-Romany gipsy. A near gipsy. One who lives like a gipsy and earns a livelihood by selling such things as clothes pegs, tins, horses, etc.

diet. In addition to the standard prison diet certain prisoners are entitled to special diets for reasons of health or religion. T.B. men get special milk and milk puddings, etc. Diabetics and vegetarians are allowed for, and Moslems, Hindus, etc., are given food in accordance with their beliefs. The Jews probably get the best deal where food is concerned and where called for by the Jewish faith they are allowed to have sent in to prison certain extra food. At Passover, for example, great quantities of food are prepared for them by one of their own faith in the prison kitchen. See *religion; Jews; T.B.; diabetics*, etc.

diet, prison. The weights allowed for various commodities naturally vary in these times, but the following is a fair average (see also *menu*):

Breakfast: A prison 'cob'—bread of about 8 oz. One pint of porridge. One pint of tea. One pat of margarine —about 3/7ths oz.

Dinner: For the most part this consists of soups. All prison meals are starchy and liquid; often supplemented with some sort of pie or dumpling. Once a week some sort of meat pie or 'hot-pot', and generally on Saturdays a bacon meal. A few prisons issue this bacon as a small rasher which many men keep to eat with their 'supper'. All bacon issues are accompanied by American or haricot beans. Fish, sometimes fried in oil saved from the cocoa, is issued every Friday. The quality of food naturally differs from prison to prison. In some prisons it may truthfully be described as *bad*, but on the whole it is as good as one should expect in such places in times of rationing. It is the monotony which causes complaints of 'bad' food. A great deal of trafficking in food goes on and this does not help the standard of meals, particularly so far as meat, bacon, sugar, tea, and other rationed commodities are concerned.

Supper: One 'cob'—a loaf of about 8 oz. One pint of tea (up to early 1948 this was a cocoa issue—see *cocoa*). One pat of margarine. One issue of sugar. Generally there is an extra of some sort. Once a week there is cheese. In season there is generally lettuce, beetroot, onions. On Sundays there is a bun or jam tart.

Cocoa: Cocoa is now issued at 8 p.m., one pint per man. This issue is now known as 'supper' and 'supper' is now referred to as 'tea'. Diets remain the same all the year round.

diet tin. The ordinary prison food pail (see *pail*). There is a shallow dish of the same metal, nowadays aluminium, which fits into the top of the tin. These tins are used only where men 'dine in' or where special diets are issued. Where men eat in association the food is brought to each table (of about twelve men) in universal cans. The new diet tins of aluminium are easier to clean than the old heavy ones, which were always greasy and which not infrequently were found to be rusty when the food had been poured out. Most 'diners in' eat from the pails in order to avoid the difficult problem of washing plates, etc.

digger. An Australian.

digger, the. Detention barracks. Service term derived from the fact that trench digging seems to be the principal occupation of men undergoing detention. See *detention; court martial; nick*, etc.

dihedral (R). The degree of dishonesty in an officer. 'What's his dihedral?' = how far is he 'bent'? does he traffic? (An obvious adaptation of R.A.F. slang.) See *bent; bent screw; fiddling; trafficking; baron.*

diner-in. In many prisons to-day men eat in the dining-halls, but there are always a few who prefer to 'dine in'. Also there are men eating in their cells for punishment—they are deprived of the advantages of association. These are called 'diners-in' and the kitchen, in making up the universal cans for the tables, allows for the number eating in cell. Their food is issued in the standard diet tin.

dining-hall. Communal living is encouraged in a number of prisons and most of these have managed to find room for separate dining-halls. In some, however, the tables are laid on the ground floor of each wing and are cleared for games and recreation after meals. Each table has a rota of orderlies who fetch the food from the kitchen, generally under the supervision of an officer or leader, and who clean up afterwards. See *association*.

dining in. Unless he is doing so at his own request, a man dining in cell is undergoing punishment. Dining in, by itself, is a minor punishment and is awarded for small breaches of rules such as untidiness at table or in cell. See *table marks*.

dip, a. A pickpocket. See also *whizz; buzz.*

Directors of Convict Prisons. Part of the Prison Commission who were responsible for convict prisons only. The Prison Commissioners attend to all matters relating to local prisons, etc. See *P.C.*

discharge. Every prisoner goes through the same routine as his day of discharge approaches. Some month or so before his date he is seen by the D.P.A. representative and, if a prisoner requiring aid, is interviewed by the N.A.D.P.A.S. board. If a convict he goes to the Central Association at Victoria, London, S.W. His clothes are inspected, he is photographed, and his finger-prints again taken. These go to the Criminal Record Office. He is interviewed by the Chaplain and the day before he actually goes out he is called up before the Governor, who explains various matters to him. He is given his papers, money, etc., on the actual morning of discharge and his clothes are pressed for him by the leader or redband in charge of reception, where he also signs for his 'property'. He also has his last prison bath and sees the Medical Officer. Prisoners and convicts are usually discharged between 7 and 7.30 a.m., though some convict prisons allow men to leave earlier and some local prisons keep them until the afternoon. The latest legal hour is about 4.30 p.m.

discharge bath. See *bath, discharge.*

disciplinary officer. An officer of the uniformed branch of the Prison Service whose sole duties are of a disciplinary nature, *i.e.* he checks and looks after halls, dining-rooms, landings; takes working parties about; looks after shops in the absence of the instructor. He also does escort duties and acts as messenger. He is not a 'tradesman' officer. See *prison officer; messenger; instructor*, etc.

divisions. The triple divisions of imprisonment are abolished by the Criminal Justice Act of 1948. In actual practice they have been ignored for many years past and all men, whether sentenced to penal servitude, imprisonment or hard labour, etc., are treated in roughly the same way. The convict has certain privileges denied the prisoner, but little by little the 'convict tradition' is being broken down. See *Criminal Justice Act*, 1948; *convict; P.S.*, etc.

do a powder. To desert from one of the services; to run away; to 'fade'. Also, *take a powder* (service).

do, to. To beat up; to thrash. Also to slash or 'chiv'. Expression recently popularised by a certain class of radio comedian. See *bashing; chiv; nutting; putting in the leather.*

64

dodgy. Anything not quite honest. Anything that has been acquired by underhand methods. Any unlawful action taken in acquiring the property of others.

dodgy grub. Stolen food. Particularly food smuggled from the prison kitchen. There is always a considerable amount of traffic in food, and many 'barons' have a standing order for weekly food. This may include half a pound or more of margarine, tea, sugar (though this commodity is more easily obtainable elsewhere), dripping (which is very popular), cooked meat, and even an occasional steak—all paid for in tobacco. See *banjo; buy; sell; baron; snout,* etc.

dog-end. Familiar old word for cigarette butt. Butts are valuable and are re-rolled over and over again. Certain jobs, such as that of office cleaner, mess waiter, outside garden party and so on have the added advantage that civilian cigarette ends are available. These are collected and if not smoked by the collector are opened up and rolled into thin 'roll-ups'. Sometimes a non-smoker has a standing arrangement with a fellow-prisoner to give him a two-ounce tin of ends for a few weekly coppers. Civilian butts have not the same value as the popular dark tobacco, except in those prisons where tobacco is hard to get because of its high price. Sometimes a considerate officer will save his ends and bring a paper bagful from home, or the local cinema, to give to a prisoner who has been helpful to him.

The health aspect is entirely overlooked by the authorities and such is the craving to smoke, having tasted the small legal amount of tobacco, that men who, outside, would shudder at the thought soon become ardent collectors of cigarette ends from all and sundry sources. See *snout; roll-up; baron; tailor-made; buy; sell,* etc.

done. Arrested; caught, having committed some offence. See *collar felt* (or *touched*); *weighed off; Follies; up the stairs*, etc.

done. Beaten up. 'So and so got done last night.' See above.

'don't want to know.' Not interested in a person or subject. 'The King returned from a foreign tour last week.'—'I don't want to know', meaning that 'I have not the slightest interest'.

dope. There seems to be an almost total absence of dope pedlars, addicts, and smugglers in local and star convict prisons and consequently slang connected with illicit drugs is negligible. The well-known 'Mary Warner' for marijuana, 'snow', or 'coke' are sometimes heard. A man who acts under the influence of drugs is referred to as being 'hopped up'.

American dope addicts, however, have their own slang. One or two words give a comparison with our own rhyming slang. An injection of any of the principal drugs is called a 'fix', or, in rhyming slang, a 'Jimmy Hix'. When the same injection is made into the artery it is called a 'main liner'. A drug addict is known as a 'hophead'.

Although little is heard about it, except when some big organisation is uncovered, there is a big drug business in England and addicts have trebled in number since the end of the war.

Drugs fall into three general classes: opium, cocaine, and marijuana. Morphine and heroin are in the same opium group. Morphine in powdered form is a fluffy, fuzzy white substance. Heroin, more granular in appearance, is white. Cocaine resembles snow, hence the common slang name. All these can be used in different ways but the hypodermic is the most popular. Opium-smoking is a complicated business, but the drug is eaten, drunk, and injected by needle. Tablets of morphine can be taken by needle or by mouth and cocaine is usually snuffed. See *vice*.

Dorchester. Local prison with about 130 cells. See *Prisons*.

dormitories. Several Borstal Institutions have no cell accommodation and all inmates live in dormitories. The system has spread to the prisons, chiefly as an answer to the overcrowding problem. Many local prisons, as well as the convict prisons for 'stars', the training establishments, etc., have converted odd rooms into dormitories. Although many men try hard to get a dormitory and prefer the communal life there are also many who prefer the privacy of the cell. In reference to prison cell accommodation in this glossary, no mention has been made of dormitories because of the constant fluctuation according to the amount of space required for other purposes. See *cell; Prisons*.

doss. To doss; to sleep. Also, *kip; flop*.

doss-house. Cheap lodging-house. A Rowton house. Also, *kip-house; flophouse*.

double lock. In most prisons the cell doors are 'double locked' or 'put on the double' when locking up for the night. They cannot then be opened by the ordinary key but only by an officer with a 'pass key'. At night this is held by the Orderly Officer. See *night screw; keys*.

D.P.A. Discharged Prisoners' Aid Societies (see also *N.A.D.P.A.S.*). About a month before discharge, a prisoner requiring help is 'called up' to appear before the N.A.D.P.A.S. Committee, who have a file of his particulars. They then decide what aid he is to be given in the way of money and employment, which is sometimes found for him before discharge.

The average prison has its D.P.A. representative,

67

a civilian unconnected with the Prison Service, although he may sometimes be a retired prison officer. He is referred to by the prisoners as 'The D.P.A.'. He interviews men on reception and towards the end of their 'time'. He keeps records of them and their needs and advises the Committee on the desirability of helping them make a fresh start. The D.P.A. also help men in their personal and family problems. It is a paid job, but where the representative is enthusiastic and sincere he can do a great deal of good and is looked on as a friend rather than a 'pest doing a job after a fashion because he is paid for it'.

Convicts are not seen by the Committee, but go to the Central Association at Victoria, London, S.W., on discharge. The D.P.A. give all men, convicts and prisoners, enough money to get them to their destinations.

Clothing is also issued by the D.P.A. to those who need it, and the local prisons were once able to carry a large stock of discarded clothing which was given to short-term men. These are given some small sum when they leave, at the most about five shillings. See *N.A.D.P.A.S.; Central Association.*

D.P.A. suit. Convicts are usually entitled to a new suit from the Central Association. This is made to measure, the tailor's shop making any necessary alterations. Many men scoff at accepting aid or a 'D.P.A.' suit, but these are usually the ones to get all they can. 'He's wearing a D.P.A. suit' is often said of a man seen leaving the prison. It is often used in a tone of derision. D.P.A. suits are generally kept in stock in the prison stores and the D.P.A. representative, where there is one, also has a private store of clothing for issue.

drag. A car or lorry. (In U.S.A.—a freight car.) 'A hot drag' = a stolen car.

drag, a. A party given by homosexuals where they all wear female clothing. See *pouff; brown hatter*, etc.

drag, to. To take a 'drag', to smoke; to draw on a cigarette. 'Give us a drag' = let me have a puff at your cigarette. It is quite common for a number of men to scrape together barely enough tobacco and dust for one cigarette, which they pass round in a circle. Perhaps one of them has a little tobacco and he passes his 'roll-up' round. As the 'owner', he is entitled to the butt, which he puts in his tin for future use with other broken-up cigarette ends. See *snout; roll-up; dog-end*.

drape. A suit of 'flashy' clothes; a 'flashy' outfit, *i.e.* Sinatra-type jacket with sports slacks. A long, American-style jacket is a 'full drape' and a short jacket a 'semi-drape'.

draughts. Games of draughts have long been permitted where men are allowed an association period. Sets of draughts may be sent in to prisoners as well as similar pastimes. See *amusements*.

drone. Hardly ever heard in prison though much popularised by the press in conjunction with 'spiv'. See *spiv*.

drop. Secret unloading place for stolen goods. Also, a tip. 'Did he drop?' = did he give you a tip? See *cop; bung, to*.

drop, long (O). Refers to the drop given to an executed man. 'The long drop', a reference to one who has been or will be executed: 'He's for the long drop.'
    A scale of drops is laid down for executioners, who also use their individual judgment. The drop given must be entered on a special form provided in a record book for executed prisoners. After execution the drop is again measured (from the gallows floor to the victim's heels) and the difference noted. Sometimes this is as much as nine inches. See *executions*.

drum. Habitation; house or room. The same as 'gaff'. 'He came round to my drum' = He visited me at home. See *gaff; Harley; rat.*

drum. Likely place to burgle. See below.

drum, dead. A house empty of occupants and ready to be burgled.

drum, live. House picked for a burglary but whose occupants, contrary to expectations, are found to be at home, thus necessitating a change of plans.

drum up. (R) Tramps' term for cooking the midday or evening stew. Also, *shackle up.*

drummer. One who thieves according to 'drumming' methods. See below.

drumming. Housebreaking or burglary though 'drumming', as distinct from 'screwing', is usually carried out during the hours of daylight and sometimes round about bedtime when, by watching (see *case*) the lights, occupied rooms can be ascertained. The daylight operation is carried out in pairs. One man rings the bell and gives some fictitious excuse if the door is opened. If the place is found empty the usual procedure is for one man to enter while the other keeps watch or cover. See *drum, dead (live); screwing,* etc.

dry lighter. Some prisons allow men to possess dry lighters and to have the special saltpetre-impregnated wick sent in by their friends or relations. It is a wise attitude to adopt, for otherwise men use the standard prison tinder box which requires tinder. To make tinder it is often necessary to destroy clothing. By permitting these harmless lighters, popular among the peasantry on the Continent, a considerable saving in clothing is achieved. See *tinder; chipper.*

drybath. A complete search of a prisoner for prohibited articles. Usually after a visit or on returning with an outside party. When a 'drybath' is given the man is stripped to the skin and the search is complete, even to a rectal examination, though this should officially be done only by the medical officer or a hospital officer. See *turnover; search; raid*, etc.

duff. No good; false (adapted from the R.A.F.). 'A duff 'Harley' = a 'phoney' club.

duff. The 'sweet' issued once or twice a week with the prisoner's dinner. The type of duff varies from prison to prison. It is sometimes described on the official menu as 'treacle pudding' and is dished out in thick, heavy wedges. Sometimes it is called 'plumduff' and has dates or figs with it. In some prisons it takes the form of a large 'dumpling' or of 'sea pie', a now obsolete concoction which resembled a soggy, untoasted muffin but which was quite pleasant to eat. Even pastry with a dab of jam or marmalade is called 'duff' when it is issued with the midday meal.

In the prison market duff always finds ready buyers and is worth from one to four 'roll-ups', according to the tobacco situation in the prison concerned. See also *diet; menu; snout; buy; sell; butter; sugar; cheese; depth-charge*, etc.

Durham. Local prison with cells for 575 men and women. See *Prisons*.

E

earliest date. All men serving prison sentences are given two dates—the actual date on which the sentence expires, and the earliest possible day of release providing the man loses no remission. These are marked on his cell card, and should he lose remission the earliest possible date is altered accordingly in red ink. See *punishments; remission*, etc.

earwig. An eavesdropper. Generally, one who uses information, overheard by eavesdropping, to curry favour with the authorities. See *grasser*.

ease it. Let up on it; go easy. In the case of 'fiddling' getting too dangerous, it is given as advice to lie low for a while.

East Sutton. East Sutton Park near Maidstone, Kent, was purchased as a freehold estate of some 85 acres with mansion and outbuildings for use as a girls' Borstal. A small party of men from Maidstone were engaged on various building and repairing projects and were accorded similar privileges to those granted to farm parties working away from prison. See *Maidstone; farm parties; Borstal Institutions; Prisons*.

'eddy.' Some men, particularly certain Londoners, have the habit of clipping their words, though here is a hint of rhyming slang: 'eddy'—ready: ready money. See also *'fick 'un'; 'fin 'un'*.

education. Of recent years a serious attempt has been made to step up the prison education scheme which has been running, after a fashion, for many years. Two prisons, Wakefield and Maidstone, are now classed as training establishments and specialise in both educational and vocational instruction. This scheme started at Wakefield, but it is safe to say Maidstone to-day is probably well ahead of other prisons in efforts to educate and to train men for fitness in the world outside. For an example of a standard educational programme in an up-to-date prison see under *Maidstone*.

Correspondence Courses: The Prison Commission have arranged for any suitable man to take up one or more free correspondence courses from among eight subjects.

This limitation of subjects is not very strictly adhered to and the B.I.E.T. who provide most of the courses (a few paid for by the Howard League are from other schools) are extremely helpful in permitting such subjects as German, Spanish, Shorthand, Plastics, Philosophy, etc. The approved eight are: Mechanical Engineering, Welding, Sheet-metal Work, General Automobile Engineering, Maintenance Engineering, General Electrical Engineering, Wiring, and Electrical Maintenance Engineering. These courses usually start with a comprehensive course in elementary and/or intermediate mathematics, which the student must complete before going on with the course proper. Building, in its various branches, is popular and numerous men have taken diplomas in various branches of Building, Engineering, etc.

In addition to correspondence courses evening classes form a big part of the educational programme in many prisons. See *Maidstone; vocational training; W.E.A.*, etc.

Education Office. In one or two prisons all classes, correspondence courses, etc., are arranged by an Education Office with a staff of three selected prisoners who are given the rank of leader (*q.v.*). These men, who are put on special trust, deal with all outside correspondence, meet potential visitors, interview all new prisoners and advise them of the programme available, keep all records, and provide the prison staff with a daily list of all men attending classes so that movement from hall to class-room can be carefully checked. These leaders work without an officer and under the direct supervision of the Governor or, sometimes, the Deputy or Assistant Governor in charge of education. See *education*, etc.

Elim choir. The Elim Evangelists are ardent entertainers at several prisons, where their choir gives frequent concerts of religious music. See *concerts*, etc.

emancipist. (O) A convict who has served his time in a penal colony. See *P.S.; lag.*

engineer. Officer, or a rank roughly equal to that of a principal officer, who is in charge of the 'Works party'. Usually promoted from a tradesman officer, he is responsible for the maintenance of the prison, the fabric, drains, gas and electrical installations, etc. The chief qualification for this important position is considerable time spent in the Prison Service and some knowledge of general works procedure. See *Works party; engineers.*

engineers. The Engineers Training Course (see *vocational training*). Also, men on the 'Works party' (*q.v.*).

envelopes. During the 1939–45 war many thousands of old envelopes were renovated for re-use by Government departments. Several prisons made contributions in this work and the 'envelope' party generally comprised the very old and the infirm men. At Wormwood Scrubs, after the war, a party of elderly and crippled men was still employed on this work. At 'tally time' they were first off the mark with the prison officers' cry of 'Lead on, Envelopes.' Graduates of Wormwood Scrubs used this cry in other prisons, as an esoteric joke, and it was always good for at least a smile.

epileptics. Men suffering from epilepsy occupy either observation cells or live in the prison hospital, from where they are permitted to go to the workshops during the daytime. See *observation cell; peephole; hospital.*

eric. *Chambers's Twentieth Century Dictionary* (1910) gives: 'blood money or the blood fine paid by a murderer to his victim's family in old Irish law. Also, Eriach, Erick.'

escape list. A list of all men who have escaped, or who have attempted or are likely to attempt to escape from prison. While a man's name is at the top of this list all special precautions are taken to minimise his chances of getting away. See *escapee*.

escapee. One who has been caught after escaping, or while preparing to escape. Such men are logged in a book (one of the many dozen kept for various purposes in all prisons) and all their movements noted separately. They are never out of the sight of an officer except when double-locked in cell and during the night their boots and clothing are put outside on a chair. They take their exercise alone, when the other men are elsewhere. See *escape list; have it away; 'one away'*, etc.

escort. Prisoners are escorted from one prison to another by officers sent from either. Frequently these officers, who are disciplinary officers and not 'tradesmen' (see *prison officer*), are harsh men when in their prisons but on escort and away from the depressing atmosphere of a gaol they change their attitude. Tobacco, cups of tea, cakes, apples, etc., are frequently provided for the travelling prisoners by their escorts.

Men attending courts during a sentence of imprisonment, or visiting sick relations (see *sick visit*), are accompanied by an escort of (officially) two officers, though often only one does this duty. If a prisoner on such a trip is lucky enough to get a 'good' officer for escort his journey can be much more pleasant.

escort, awaiting. Frequently a man serving a sentence passed by a civil court has another charge awaiting him and he is 'picked up' at the prison gate by the police and rearrested. If he is expecting this, and legally he should be warned within a certain period before his discharge, he is referred to as 'awaiting escort'.

Men serving civil sentences often have military charges against them and the service concerned sends an escort of it's M.P.'s to 'pick the man up' at the gate on the day of his discharge. This happens quite frequently, mostly with men wanted for desertion. See *court martial.*

executions. Almost any county paper has on its files detailed accounts of executions carried out towards the end of the last century and at the beginning of this. Nowadays an execution passes almost unnoticed by the press. Although some of the old customs have fallen into disuse the actual carrying out of the sentence of death has altered very little in the past eighty years or so. The black flag and the tolling bell are gone. The number of people attending an execution is limited to the smallest possible and the utmost privacy is accorded the condemned man.

Wearing a uniform fitted with tapes instead of buttons (which might be swallowed), the sentenced man spends his 'three clear Sundays' in the condemned cell (see *C.C.*), watched day and night by two officers (see *death watch*). Any desire to commit suicide is earnestly discouraged. He sleeps with his hands above the bedclothes (so no concealed razor can slash an artery); his smoking is limited for the sake of his health; and special meals (see *C.C.*) are prepared and served by the officer cook. He takes his exercise in a yard where none but his guards can see him.

One day the executioner comes and takes a peep at him through the Judas and, the man's weight, height, and type of neck being known, is able to calculate the drop necessary for a neat job of work.

The heavy doors of the gallows-trap fall back against pads to deaden the sound and protect them. They are too heavy to bounce back against a falling body. Prisoners working in the vicinity of the 'topping shed' claim to have heard the dull crash of these heavy trapdoors when the hangman has tested his release with the aid of a sack weighted to equal the weight of the condemned man.

On the morning of an execution all men are locked in their cells and as a rule the clocks are stopped. This practice is now falling into disuse, because men imprisoned at the time of a hanging claim to be able to judge the exact moment, and on such a morning there is an air of suppressed excitement and depression, when the whole prison is enveloped in the silence of the grave.

According to numerous officers, who appreciate the duties of the death watch, quite a number of men do eat the much popularised 'last breakfast' and make a valiant effort to put on a good show of bravery. Few need support and the majority give the impression that the final arrival of the fatal hour is a great relief after the long wait in close confinement.

The Chaplain enters the condemned cell and attends to any spiritual requirements of the man, after which the hangman, Governor, and Medical Officer enter with the Sheriff. The hangman may be accompanied by an assistant, perhaps a student in the art of hanging. He meets his 'client', holds out a hand as if in greeting, and, taking the man by surprise, puts on a 'half-nelson' which allows him to secure the wrists behind the back.

With an officer on each side, a firm hand gripping the upper arm, he is whisked from the condemned cell, along a frequently very short passage, through the double swing doors of the 'topping shed', and in a matter of seconds is standing on the chalk mark on the trapdoors. The hangman, or his assistant, stoops to secure the ankles with a strap.

The noose hangs level with the head, the slack supported by a thread from the stout cross beam. Noose and hood are slipped over the collar-and-tieless neck and head. A nod from the hangman and the officers step aside to ledges clear of the trapdoors and remain standing holding side rails let into the walls. For a split second the man stands alone; perhaps a gentle slap on the buttocks and a grim 'so long'; the hangman springs the trap and, according to the supporters of capital punishment, death is instantaneous.

A formal inquest is then held in the Governor's office and the man is left hanging for an hour. The Medical Officer has been down into the pit, certified death, and severed the arteries. A notice is posted outside the prison gates to the effect that the sentence of the court has been carried out. Such is the morbid nature of many people that even the most unimportant murderer commands a crowd at the gates on the morning of his execution. Those murders which make the big headlines draw great crowds to the gates on the morning of the last scene. There is no doubt that public hangings, were they to be revived, would rival dog-racing in popularity. In the United Kingdom public executions were abolished on 11 May 1868.

The hangman, having measured the distance of the drop after execution, has finished his work. The difference in drop before and after varies considerably. Measured from the level of the gallows floor to the bottom of the man's heels the difference is sometimes as much as nine inches. There have even been cases where a miscalculation is said to have caused severance of the head. The neck has frequently proved stronger than allowed for, with the result that death has been due to asphyxia. This point is allowed for in the final records.

A number of grim details must then be entered in the Record of Executions Book and, if available, a cutting from the local press is pasted on the opposite page.

The Governor and Medical Officer certify below the hangman's name and address that they consider him a fit person to perform such duties and, if such is the case, that the execution was carried out with all expedition and skill. Should the hangman show signs of having imbibed rather too freely on arrival at the prison, this is duly noted against him.

Next to the details of the executed man the Medical Officer certifies the cause of death, which, according to the printed form in the Record Book, may be due to '(a) fracture of the vertebræ or (b) asphyxia'. From this, one may deduce that it cannot be proved conclusively that death by hanging is instantaneous.

The duty of providing a grave falls on the Engineer Officer in charge of the Works. He duly appoints officers to dig the grave. On the last morning a screen is placed round this while the coffin is placed ready for the arrival of the Chaplain to read the last rites.

Although it is customary to inter executed men in lime (provision for ordering this is made in the store books: 'Lime—for executed prisoners'), it has been found that in certain soils it has a preserving effect and consequently charcoal is sometimes used instead. The coffin is perforated to assist decomposition.

Legally an executed man must be buried in an unmarked grave 'in the precincts of the prison in which he was last confined' (see *death sentence*). It is often an unofficial custom to mark, if not the name, at least the date, in the brick of the wall beside the grave. In one prison rude cement 'tablets' bearing the name and date of execution were long visible, but a recent Governor had them all removed. In many prisons, however, it is still possible to see, in some forgotten corner, a shrub-covered patch where no one goes and where hanged men were once lowered into the lime. See *C.C.; death watch; hangman; topping shed; gallows*, etc.

exercise. There are two official periods for exercise, each of about thirty minutes' duration. This exercise consists of walking round and round a narrow cement path. In local prisons there are three paths. The inner one reserved for cripples and old men, who may amble along in their own time; the centre is used by debtors, etc.; and the main outer ring is filled with a line of hurrying 'ordinary' prisoners. Lavatories are placed beside each exercise yard and men are expected to make use of them during this period. They are generally full of 'dodgers' trying to get a quick smoke by sitting with their heads below the top of the half-doors.

At one time smoking was allowed only on exercise and gas jets were provided for the purpose of obtaining a light. Remands, for example, were not allowed to smoke in cell and on coming out for exercise were given one cigarette. When this was finished they could obtain another (sent in by their friends) from the warder on duty. At the end of the period the last cigarette butt had to be surrendered. A fresh cigarette could be obtained only by the surrender of a butt. To-day the rules are reversed and, except at Christmas time, no smoking is allowed during exercise.

This monotonous round of 'exercise' is one of the most soul-destroying parts of prison life. Particularly so when badly made prison shoes are issued (see *shoes*, etc.). The tedium is largely relieved nowadays by men being allowed, in some prisons, to exercise in pairs and thus be able to talk. Remands must keep single file and talking is strictly against regulations. In some modern prisons exercise is taken round the paths and roads of the prison grounds, and, of course, in the open-camp prisons it is not necessary, as men are free to roam at will within the defined limits. See *yards; lavatories*.

Exeter. Local prison for men and women with accommodation for 241.

eye eye. Look out. Have a look round. Keep your eyes open. See *nit nit; case*, etc.

F

fag. Cigarette. See *snout; tab; butt; roll-up; tailor-made*, etc.

fairy. See *pouff; pansy; brown hatter*.

farm parties. Parties working on farms, etc., away from the prison (see above) are usually chosen from men nearing the end of their sentences. These parties take a certain amount of food with them and, with what the farmer gives them or what they can 'scrounge', they prepare a midday meal. On returning to the prison in the evening, however, they are given the normal prison dinner in addition to the usual 'tea' or 'supper'. As a rule these men are given a little extra tobacco at the end of the week, about half an ounce each. This is given by the farmer out of his own pocket and in addition he pays the Commissioners full rate for every man. It is a constant source of grouse with the men that they do not benefit financially and the extra tobacco is given as an inducement to good work. Prisoners are not entitled to the allowance of extra food given to ordinary farm workers. Farmers, on the whole, appreciate the work done by prisoners and farm parties have proved a great success. See *camps, farm; open camp prisons*, etc.

farm, prison. A number of prisons have their own farms, on which they produce food for both consumption in the prison and for sale outside. Supervised by prison officers, or a 'civilian' bailiff, these farms are worked entirely by prisoners. Other prisons send out parties of men to work for local farmers, or for the W.A.E.C., etc. See below.

Feltham. Borstal Institution with accommodation for 422. Men from this establishment farm land acquired at Stanwell as a site for a women's prison. See *Borstal Institutions; Prisons; Stanwell.*

fence. Receiver of stolen property. See *granny; swordsman,* etc.

fenders. Ships' fenders, made of rope, which are a product of many prison bagshops. See *mailbags; cell tasks,* etc.

'fick 'un.' Thick one. 'Thick 'un.' A thick or well-rolled cigarette with enough tobacco in it to give a good smoke. As distinct from the all-too-common thin roll-ups which are the customary prison 'currency'. See *'eddy'; snout; 'fin 'un'.*

fiddling. Begging or scrounging. An illegal, shady transaction, involving more than one person. Transactions of which the authorities are well aware but which they are unable—or perhaps unwilling—to stop. Providing no actual harm is done, a blind eye is generally turned on minor fiddling; so long as the men remain contented and well disciplined. Ninety-nine per cent. of all prison 'fiddling' involves tobacco. See *snout; buy; sell; traffic,* etc.

films. Most big prisons own a 16-mm. sound projector on which are shown weekly films. These are generally supplied by the Ministry of Information, but about once a month the average prison is able to put on a feature film. Feature films, 'Mutiny of the Bounty', the Marx Brothers, 'Charlie Chan', are good old regulars, and are supplied from prison funds (if any). The Salvation Army are exceptionally good at lending gangster and other pictures; also one or two other social organisations help in this direction. See *amusements; concerts.*

filter. To desert. 'Brassed off with the army, I just filtered' = fed up, I deserted. See *trot, on the; run, on the; escort; court martial.*

'fin 'un.' A thin one. A very thin 'roll-up' (*q.v.*). Most traffickers in roll-ups sell only very thin cigarettes, which are gone in a puff or two. See also *'fick 'un'; eddy.*

Findlay, a (M). A prisoner who buys tobacco, makes it all into thin, hand-rolled cigarettes ('roll-ups'), and sells them separately. Thus he is able to make a profit which will allow him to buy a larger quantity of tobacco on the following week.

The word 'Findlay' is little used; 'baron' is still the popular prison name, even though, like the word 'spiv' (*q.v.*), it has achieved popularity in a certain section of the popular press.

Half an ounce of shag-type tobacco will give about thirty-odd cigarettes which can be sold at a penny each. After the 1947 Budget half an ounce of cheap shag cost 1s. 8d. Thus it was necessary to sell twenty cigarettes at one penny each to pay for the cost of production. Out of the profit has to come a margin for bad debts. Non-payers frequently get rough treatment from the 'barons' or, more generally, their paid strong-arm men (see *baron*).

Only the 'mugs' and the very impatient buy 'roll-ups', for they rarely give a smoke of any satisfaction and are gone in a few puffs. In a few prisons (in pre-Budget days) halfpenny 'roll-ups' were obtainable, but these were made mostly of civilian cigarette ends, collected from the 'gate' or the Officers' Mess, broken up, mixed with dust and even scraps of the paper, and sold to those who were not likely to complain.

There are always 'mugs' and that is why the 'Findlays', be they honest or 'bent', are successful.

At Maidstone an experiment, which proved successful,

83

was tried out to thwart the 'Findlays' and 'barons'. Each evening the Principal Officer in charge of the hall made 'roll-ups' available at a penny each. These could be bought on credit up to six in number and were available to all men earning less than tenpence a week. With tenpence a man could buy a quarter of an ounce on 'snout day' and it was considered that such men could wait. Those earning less than that sum seldom have the patience to save their money for two or three weeks in order to buy a quarter or half an ounce.

A 'Findlay' has to be a careful judge of men if he is to succeed and with a little business acumen he can soon be classed a 'baron'. See *snout; roll-up; tailor-made; baron; trafficking*, etc.

finished. 'What finished you?' = what was the cause of your being caught? how did you get caught? See *do; done; weighed off; cased*, etc.

fire party. Small parties of prisoners are detailed to act as fire parties in the event of fire breaking out in the prison. Periodical practices are held under the supervision of a 'Works' officer. During World War II prisoners formed A.R.P. parties.

firearms (see *arms*). The carrying of firearms is frowned on by the 'genuine burglar'. Among the young prison population, inspired by lurid literature and American gangster films, a great deal of romance seems to be attached to the possession of a revolver (see *rod; Roscoe; heater*); and the shoulder holster and turned-down brim are looked on as the hall-mark of 'toughness'.

first bird. First time in prison. Doing his 'first bird', or first imprisonment. See *time*.

first timer. One doing his 'first bird'.

84

fish day. Fish is probably the most unpopular meal of the week and many a prisoner counts the number of 'fish days' to go before the end of his sentence. See *U.S. day*.

fitters party. The Engineering Course party. See *vocational training*.

fixed. 'How are you fixed?' = how well off are you in tobacco or money?

flash. Showy; 'ritzy'. Also used as a nickname for one who is, or thinks he is, 'smart' or cunning. See *Flash Jimmy*.

Flash Jimmy. 'He's a Flash Jimmy' = he likes to overdress and to throw his money around. A 'spiv' is generally a Flash Jimmy. See *spiv*, etc.

flattie (M). Policeman. This refers only to a uniformed policeman or to one who, even in civilian clothes, bears the unmistakable mark of the foot patrolman. See *cop; bogey*, etc.

flim. Five-pound note; five pounds. See *cow; calf; nicker; crackle*, etc.

flim. A sentence of five years' penal servitude. Also, *handful*.

flints. Lighter flints and cigarette papers are among the articles which men are permitted to have 'sent in'. Although only 'dry lighters' are permitted in the best prisons, a blind eye is turned on the use of tinder boxes, which are found in every type of prison. A few prisons permit, or even issue, matches, but the tinder is the recognised means of obtaining a light. Ordinary lighter flints, or better still the large gas-lighter type, are inserted in the end of a small piece of wood. This is usually about an inch cut off the end of a prison pen.

By striking the flint sharply with a scrap of razor blade a spark is obtained See *tinder box; chipper*.

flock. Flock is used only for mattresses and pillows made specially for officers. For prisoners coir is used. Flock is also used by hobbies classes engaged in making 'soft' toys. See *coir; mattresses; bagshop*.

flophouse. Occasionally used by those young men who affect Americanisms. See *doss-house*.

flowers. In the High Court at the Old Bailey it is still the custom that flowers are placed before the Judge at the opening of the day's hearing. This dates from the time when herbs were brought into court to help stifle the stench from the crowd. See *herbs*.

Flowers have a great attraction for many prisoners, as have animals and children. This is only natural considering the almost planned ugliness with which the majority of them are surrounded. Men will go to great trouble and take considerable risks (of three days' bread and water, in some cases) to obtain, if not cultivated flowers, then wild ones or colourful weeds. In the better prisons this is actually encouraged. Vases are made from old jam jars, tins, and sometimes from moulded wax stolen from the 'bagshop'.

flowery. 'Flowery' and 'Peter' are the two most popular words used for the prison cell. They originate from the old song 'Peter Bell'. Flowery dell provides rhyming slang for cell. See *Peter; cell*.

flue (R). Prison officer. Rhyming slang for 'screw'. See *screw*, etc.

fluff. Young girl. Any woman who tries to look younger than she really is and who overdoes it. See *tart*.

Follies (M). Quarter Sessions. 'To be weighed off at the Follies' = tried at the Quarter Sessions. See *up the stairs*.

follow-up wagon. Motorised police who follow up a raid with reinforcements. The 'heavy stuff'. See *Sweeney; holler wagon; heavy stuff.*

food orderly. The hall cleaners are also responsible for carrying the food from the kitchen to the landings, where it is handed to men in their cells by an officer. Where men eat in association, each table has an orderly who, with the table leader, collects the food for that table. He also cleans up afterwards and returns the empty tins to the kitchen. This duty is taken in turn. Frequently the men on a table subscribe a penny a week each to one man who keeps the job permanently. See *table leader.*

form. A man 'with form' is one with a criminal record, one with previous convictions. Such men have to be extra careful, as their finger-prints are recorded and they are often known to the police by sight.

fountain pens. Because of their value in the 'black market', fountain pens are prohibited, even in the training centres. See *pens and ink; letters.*

F.P. False pretences; obtaining money by fraud. See also *R.W.V.; G.B.H.,* etc.

frisk. To search. Another common expression popular with the young man who likes to affect Americanisms. See *rubdown; drybath; turnover.* Also, *gat; broad.*

Fry, Elizabeth. Eighteenth-century prison reformer. Founded the first Women's Visiting Committee to women in Newgate. Like her male counterpart Howard, Mrs. Fry was too busy reforming to cope with her own children, but her work has long been remembered and appreciated. See *N.A.P.V.*

fuel economy. On the centre of many prisons the 'Fuel Economy Board' may still be seen. An old bedboard, painted black, this was used for recording the weekly consumption of fuel and indicated the amounts saved. No doubt it was watched with considerable interest by prisoners serving winter sentences during the war. See *heating*.

full sheet. A report against an officer for an offence of some seriousness. See *half sheet; got the book*.

fumigator. The fumigator is in charge of the P.W.S. (*q.v.*). All clothing and bedding from cells where men suffering from infectious diseases have been housed are fumigated here.

furniture, cell. Each cell contains a bedboard or one of the newer 'hammock beds' which are replacing the old wooden board (see *beds, spring*). A coir-stuffed mattress and pillow are part of the equipment (see *reception kit*). There is a fixed wall-table just inside the door, under the light. Though to-day many cells have the light in the middle of the ceiling, the position of this table, of great thickness, is determined by the fact that for many years the only lighting was by a gas jet let into the wall at table level and protected by a sheet of glass (see *gas; lighting*). There is a triangular washstand with enamelled bowl, jug, shaving mug, soap-dish and chamber pot (this last with or without lid and nowadays mostly without a handle). A small dustpan is provided and at one time there was a small prison-made rope brush for sweeping the floor. In many prisons these have been withdrawn and men collect a broom from the landing orderly (see *cleaning materials*). Where a man eats in his cell (see *diner-in*). an enamelled plate, a china mug, and knife, fork, and spoon are provided; also an earthenware salt cellar which he fills from a box of salt on the centre. The knife is usually made of tin, but in most prisons these are collected after each meal. There is usually a strip of coconut matting on the board or slate floor. See *cell layout; cell; bedding; bathing kit; slates*, etc.

G

Gabriel (R). Nickname given to the chapel organist. See *redband*.

gadie. Gipsy word for one who is not a Romany. A man. See *didikai*.

gaff. The most common prison word for a dwelling-place, house, or room. 'They did him in his gaff' = they arrested him at home. 'He screwed a gaff' = he robbed a house. (Early English thieves' cant.) See *drum; rat; screw, to*.

gaff, gambling. A gaming-house. See *schpieler*.

gaffer. The 'boss'. The officer or leader in charge of a working-party.

galley. Cookhouse or kitchen.

gallows. Popularly visualised as a post with a right-angled beam projecting at the top; situated on some windswept moor or lonely cross-roads. A gallows differs from a *gibbet* (*q.v.*) in that gallows are used for hanging a man until he is dead. The 'modern' gallows, such as those used in the 'hanging or topping prisons' of to-day, is somewhat different. The gallows shed is usually situated within a few steps of the condemned cell. It is small and dark. The floor is mostly taken up with the heavy double trapdoors. On each side is a space for the officers to stand on, gripping a handrail let into the wall, while the prisoner is alone for a last brief moment. Overhead, from wall to wall, is a stout beam from which hangs the rope, the slack held by a thin thread. Entrance is through double doors with a triple lock. Separate keys are held by the Governor, Chief

Officer and Engineer Officer; and the room cannot be opened without all three being present, except for special occasions or when, perhaps, the Engineer Officer, who is responsible for the burial of the hanged, admits the hangman for purposes of preparing the gallows for use. See *executions*.

gambling. Although all gambling and betting is, naturally, strictly forbidden in H.M. prisons there are always the inveterate gamblers who will find something on which to stake their money or tobacco.

Nearly every prison has its bookmaker, who often makes a very good thing out of his business. He takes bets on all the big races, boxing matches, dog races, and so on, as well as on local events such as inter-hall football games, races on Sports Day, and on indoor games such as darts, table tennis, etc. He is usually at the head of any move to run organised football pools, for which coupons have actually been printed in prison, and he usually makes a practice of paying out in full 'on the dot'. Thus he is able to establish himself. Frequently the bookmaker is a non-smoker and his motives for making money may be because he intends to 'take out' as much as he can; and there is a great deal of money to be made in prison by a 'smart man'. On the other hand, it may be an inherent business instinct which he cannot stifle and which finds an outlet by such activities. Strange to say, it is not uncommon to find such a man, who is perhaps the leading 'baron', with an extremely generous heart. Such men 'buy' food from a man who is anxious for a smoke, and then, when the man has lit his smoke, return the butter or sugar or whatever it was. Such a man can usually be trusted in many ways and is a refreshing type to meet in the usual squalor of prison life.

Many men gamble on paper only. Studying racing results, and keeping a book, they calculate what they 'could have won' had they actually betted outside. These men are frequently in prison because of money difficulties caused by gambling. They rarely bet in prison and remain convinced that 'next time' they cannot fail to make huge sums. See *amusements; cards; baron; snout; bookmaker*, etc.

gambling gaff. A gaming-house. See *gaff*.

gander. To look. 'Have a gander' = to look around or at anything. See *darry*.

gannet. Any glutton. Any prisoner (though it may refer to any officer) who is always routing round the food pails for left-over food. (From the bird of the Boobies family, the Solan Goose.) Every dining-hall has its 'gannet' and frequently there is one at every table. It has been known for all the men on a table to back their 'gannet' against another from an adjoining table. The bet may be on how many plates of porridge one 'gannet' can put away at a sitting and all men on his table forfeit their porridge to help in the contest. Frequently the promoters standing by blow on the steaming plates, while the contestants shovel away at the cool edges, moving from plate to plate and back again as the porridge cools off. Hall officers, however, are apt to frown on such exhibitions.

gardens. Garden space is usually very limited, but what is not cultivated for the kitchen is carefully tended by the garden party, and in some prisons where there is more space plots are allotted to individual men. Sometimes the chapel orderly is in charge of certain beds, in which he takes great pride. The National Gardens Guild has been of great help in providing, where possible, lecturers and in sending gifts of plants and bulbs to prisons. Wealthy prisoners have, in the past, made extremely beautiful gardens out of waste plots by having the necessary bulbs, seeds, and plants 'sent in'.

Unfortunately some of these have suffered because of the keen gardening instincts of some officers, who have not hesitated to take bulbs, cuttings, plants, etc., to their own gardens.

garotte. Old Spanish custom of strangulation. The victim wears a brass collar fitted with a thumbscrew, the point of which pierces the spinal marrow. Also spelt 'garrotte' (Spanish: 'garrote').

gas. Even to-day there are prisons lighted exclusively by gas and it has been found necessary to re-install certain gas fittings in case of electricity cuts. Cells were originally lighted by gas jets set in a niche cut in the wall by the fixed corner table. A sheet of thick glass was placed between prisoner and the jet, which was lighted from the corridor. These jets helped to warm the cells. In nearly all prison halls the main gas fittings remain and are frequently used to save electricity. In the dining and association rooms there is always a small gas jet from which men may light their cigarettes. These jets are lighted by the officer in charge, at the official start of the smoking period. See *lighting; tinder*, etc.

gash. Spare. 'Have you any gash coppers?' (service).

gat. American slang, probably out of use in the U.S.A., but used by youths who affect Americanisms. The English slang for revolver is *heater*, for pistol, *Roscoe*.

gate. Any door or gate in the prison. 'Gate, please' is the call a leader gives to an officer when he wishes that official to open the door to let him out of a hall. Officers not carrying keys also use this call to other officers who are on duty, 'Gate, sir'. The officer in charge then comes over with his keys.

gate, the. The main gate through which pass all who enter or leave a prison. Here are the 'Gate Officer's' cubby-hole, waiting-room for visitors, officer's rest or waiting-room, and the dreary little visiting boxes. There are two gates to all old prisons. The outer, set in a high arch, is of oak and iron; the inner of huge iron bars. All vehicles entering or leaving first pass through one, which is locked before the other is opened. Never may both gates be unlocked at the same time. See *keys; gate screw; visits*, etc.

gate fever. Nervous excitation at the approaching day of discharge. Some prisoners get this trouble long before they are actually due for discharge. With others it is not felt until a day or two before the awaited day and often it does not come at all or comes weeks before discharge, disappears, and a feeling of anticlimax is felt on the last morning. Gate fever is a very real thing and Medical Officers recognise its importance on the general bearing and behaviour of a prisoner. See also *debtor's colic; cobitis; whanker's doom.*

gate screw. The officer on duty at the main gate. Although there is a roster for this duty there is usually at least one officer for whom it is a whole-time job. He is more often than not an old-time regular and he never takes any duty in the prison proper. He is in charge of the keys and keeps a record of all who enter and leave. See *keys; screw.*

G.B.H. Grievous bodily harm. 'He's a G.B.H. man' = he is in prison on a charge of violence. See also *F.P.; R.W.V.*

gear. Swag, haul. This word is used far more than is 'swag'. 'They did him with his gear' = he was arrested with his swag. See *swordsman*, etc.

gee. To put in the 'G'. To exert pressure. (From 'g', gravity—R.A.F. slang.) To give information to the authorities about a fellow-prisoner. See also *bubble; grass, to.*

93

gee-er. One who puts in the 'G'. A trouble-maker. One who tells lies about another in order to provoke a fight. In this sense 'gee-er' is in common use. 'He "gee-ed" them up' = he provoked them into a quarrel. See also *bubble; tube; grasser; gee.*

geezer. The very common word for a person. A 'bloke'. Anyone of the lower or middle classes. 'Old geezer' = old man (or woman). See *Pop.*

gessein (M). To 'con'. See *con; gessump; gesseiner,* etc.

gesseiner. Valuables. Possessions. Belongings. See *gessump.*

gesseiner. In the Merchant Navy this means a garbage can.

gessump. To acquire the possessions of another by 'conning' (working the confidence game), or by stealing. To 'gessump the gesseiner' = to steal, or otherwise acquire illegally, the possessions of another. See *con; gesseiner; gessein.*

'get your back scratched.' To get the cat-o'-nine-tails. See *corporal punishment; cat; pussy; tickler; scratched; apron.*

gibbet. Form of gallows on which criminals were once exhibited after execution (*v.t.,* to expose on a gibbet). See *gallows; executions.*

Gladstone Committee. Until a publication of 1945, *Prisons and Borstals,* issued by the Home Office, there had been no official prison policy expressed since the Report of the Gladstone Committee in 1895. See *Criminal Justice Act,* 1948.

glasses. Glasses are provided free to those prisoners requiring them. See *dentists; hospital,* etc.

glory, got the. 'He's got the glory' = he's got religion. One who has suddenly turned religious while serving a sentence. Sometimes spoken of as having 'got the Book'. In every prison there are a small number of fawning sycophants who profess conversion to one or other of the faiths but who are really weak and frightened or are men who just 'can't take it'. Others imagine that by 'crawling' round the chaplain or priest they will get preferential treatment. Both these types make the chaplain's task more difficult, but they are usually easy to see through and to weed out from a few who are sincere in their beliefs. See *chapel*, etc.

Gloucester. Local prison with accommodation for 217. See *Prisons*.

go for a slash, to. To visit the urinal. See *karzy*, etc.

God Man, the (R). The prison chaplain (service slang).

Golden Glory (R). Nickname, from a brand of soap, for the bath-house orderly in some prisons. See *bath leader*, etc.

got the Book. 'He's got the Book' has two meanings, (*a*) he has 'got' religion or (*b*) that an officer has been suspended from duty pending a serious charge, such as trafficking. When an officer is reported by a Principal Officer he gets 'a half sheet', that is, the report is made out on a small form roughly half a sheet in size. A 'full sheet' is a bigger form, allowing for more detail, so that he's 'got the book' means he has the biggest possible report against him. See *half sheet; full sheet.*

Governor. A new type of Governor is now coming into the Prison Service and the old hard-bitten ex-officer type has had his day. It is a constant source of discontent among the uniformed branch that the average warder stands practically no chance of promotion to

Governor. On the whole this is a very good thing. Only if promotion is quick could such a thing be of value in a system which calls for much more than the mere locking and unlocking of doors. The new Governors and Assistant Governors, if elevated from the lower ranks, should be men in the prime of life, unsoured by years of monotony, so that every scrap of initiative possessed should be utilised to the greatest advantage. The present new intakes come from the officer class and, for the most part, are men with zeal and an awareness of the social importance of their jobs. On these men depends the success of a new era in prison reform.

Governor's clerk. A member of the clerical staff. The Governor's clerk acts as his secretary and works in liaison with the Steward. See *clerical staff; prison officer.*

G.P.O. During the war a great deal of work was done for the G.P.O. by prisoners. As an example, Wormwood Scrubs and other prisons had parties of men engaged in assembling various telephone components and dismantling broken and obsolete apparatus. Mailbags, etc., are also made on contract with the G.P.O.

grab. Pay. See *lob; grab day.*

grab day. Pay day. See *pay; lob; grab.*

granny. A legitimate business used as a cover to nefarious activities, particularly to that of fence. See *fence; swordsman.*

grapevine. Fact or rumour passed from one to another by word of mouth. The 'underground' route for information.

grass, to. To betray another by giving information to the authorities. To 'squeal'. This is one of the most commonly used slang words in prison to-day. See *grasser.*

grasser. One who gives information. A 'squealer' or 'squeaker'. The origin derives from rhyming slang: grasshopper—copper; a 'grass' or 'grasser' tells the 'copper' or policeman. (Also, a policeman.)

gravy, dishing out the. During Quarter Sessions or Assizes, when a Judge is giving heavy sentences, he is spoken of as 'dishing out the gravy (or porridge)'. Thus, 'Cor, he ain' arf dishin' aht the porridge.' Meaning that, to the speaker, he appears to be giving heavy and excessive sentences to all who appear before him.

greatcoat. The greatcoat or overcoat is rarely issued in prison. Its place is taken by the regulation prison cape which hangs to about waist level (see *cape*). A very short greatcoat is sometimes issued to elderly or invalid men who live in hospital and who need this on exercise. A few such coats may be seen at Parkhurst.

greentie. A "leader" (*q.v.*) in a women's star prison.

greyband. In a convict prison a convict who has reached the 'special' stage. At four years he is given a grey band to wear on each cuff of his blue coat, denoting four years' good conduct and entitling him to all the privileges of a 'special'. See *stage; Special.*

greycoat. The ordinary prisoner, from the grey uniform of the local prisons and for convicts who have not reached the second 'stage'. See *stage; bluecoat; ordinaries.*

greys, the. The 'greybands' or 'special' stage men, spoken of collectively. See above.

griddle. To busk, or sing in the street. See *chant; busker.*

griffin. The 'gen'. The right information. 'Give me the griffin' = tell me all about it (service slang).

grub. The common word for any sort of food. See *diet; menu.*

Guv, the. The prison Governor. See *light of love; dep.; corned beef; screwdriver.*

gymnastics. Although P.T. classes, providing they involve only the lightest exercises and the bars, horse, etc., are not used, may be conducted by a suitable prisoner, gymnastics may only be indulged in when a qualified instructor is present. Qualified P.T. instructors are generally to be found among the officers, and in 1945 the Central Council of Physical Recreation organised a course for P.T. instructors in the Prison Service. See *P.T.*

gyves (O). Old-fashioned word for shackles or fetters, no longer seen in our prisons. See *chains.*

H

haircut. Any very short term of imprisonment. In a local prison, one or two months or weeks. In a convict prison, three to five years. See *time; lagging*, etc.

hair-oil. There is always a good demand for hair-oil among that section of the prison population which tries to keep itself extra smart. The most easily obtained is machine oil from the tailor's shop and sometimes vaseline which is used for greasing certain types of machine thread, etc. Liquid paraffin is much sought after and can sometimes be obtained by reporting 'sick'. Olive oil is occasionally obtainable through the Officers' Mess or the R.C. Chapel. The 'Brylcreem Boys' will even use the prison margarine ration and have little respect for the pillow-slips which later have to be used by others. See *barber; buy; sell; fiddling*, etc.

half a bar. Ten shillings. See *calf; bar; cow; nicker; pony; white; flim; crackle*, etc.

half a century. Fifty pounds. A century is one hundred of anything; generally, though, it refers to pounds sterling. Also, 'half a ton', 'half a hundred'.

half a chip. Sixpence. See *chip; sparsie.*

half a cock. Five pounds (from rhyming slang, cock and hen—ten). See *flim; crackle; cock and hen.*

half a hundred. Fifty pounds. See above.

half a nicker. Ten shillings. See *nicker; half a bar.*

half a stretch. Six months' imprisonment. See *stretch; time,* etc.

half-brass. A girl or woman who associates freely with men but who does not accept money in return for her favours. See *brass; tart; broad.*

half-iron. One who associates with homosexuals but who is not actually abnormal himself. See *iron; pouff; brown hatter; drag,* etc.

half-sheet. An officer reported by a superior is given a half-sheet of blank paper on which to explain his conduct See *full sheet; got the book.*

hall. The cell blocks. See *landing,* etc.

hall leader. The leader who is responsible for keeping a particular hall or cell block clean. He also runs errands for the officer in charge, supervises all cleaners' work on his landings (one cleaner per landing), and collects food from the kitchen. He keeps the roll of men located in his hall, arranges the changing of sheets, pillow-slips, etc., and issues games sets during association period. He is responsible for the general tidiness and smooth-running of his hall and is in a position to be of great help to the men living in his hall. See *leader; stage; table leader.*

99

hammock. The hammocks used on board ship. These are made in some prison bagshops and are sometimes issued as cell tasks. See *mailbags; cell task.*

hammock bed. The old-fashioned bedboard is slowly being replaced by the canvas 'hammock' type of bed. It consists of a metal frame, rather like the wartime A.R.P. stretcher, with short legs and has canvas stretched across it by a cord run through brass eyelets. A standard prison mattress is used with this type of bed. Rubber tips are bolted to the legs to prevent wearing away the floor. See *bedboard; furniture, cell; beds, spring.*

handful. Five years' penal servitude. See *time.* Also, five pounds. See *flim; crackle; half a cock,* etc.

handicrafts. Experiments in some prisons have introduced such handicrafts as weaving, rug-making, leather work, modelling, pottery, and so on. These occupations are purely voluntary and are extremely popular. See *education; hobbies; Maidstone.*

handle. Christian name, nickname, or surname. Usually a surname. It can also refer to titles or degrees or other qualifications.

hangman. Executioner who holds public office. From time to time the popular press gives publicity to the private life of the current hangman. After the late war the official executioner was busy in Germany, working with the American hangmen, disposing of condemned war criminals. The carpenter's shop in at least one British prison was kept busy making special boxes to contain the equipment necessary for a hanging. These boxes were destined for Nuremberg.

Before an English execution the hangman arrives at the prison the night before the hanging and sleeps within the prison walls. He may not bring into the prison any alcohol or drug and thus it is assured that the task is performed by a man whose mind is not muddled by drink. After the hanging the Governor and Medical Officer make a joint report on the way in which he carried out his job. See *executions*.

hard labour. Dates from the days of the treadmill and shot drill. All divisions of imprisonment have been abolished by the Criminal Justice Act of 1948. Although the terms 'hard labour', 'penal servitude', etc., have been in use for many years, they have long ceased to have any real meaning. All men, prisoners and convicts alike, receive similar treatment. See *Criminal Justice Act*, 1948; *divisions*.

Harley, a. A club. A 'duff' Harley = a club that is no good—phoney.

have it away. To escape. See *over the wall; 'one away'; scarper*.

H.B.I. Housebreaking implements. It is illegal to carry certain instruments such as a *'loid (q.v.)*, glass-cutter, jemmy, or wire keys, etc. A man with *form (q.v.)* takes a grave risk carrying such instruments. A question of great importance to painters was raised when a painter was arrested for being in possession of a diamond cutter, a tool essential to his particular job. See *R.W.V.; F.P.*, etc.

heading. Using the top of the head in a fight, by butting the opponent in the face. See also *nutting; putting in the leather; do, to*, etc.

heater. Revolver. This word is the English equivalent of 'gat' or 'rod', expressions used by those who affect Americanisms. See *Roscoe; arms*.

heating. All prison heating arrangements are uneconomical. Some of the old local prisons are heated from a huge fire in the centre of the lower landing, usually below ground level. This is stoked with coke and the noise at night is terrific with the scrape of shovels on the stone or slate floors. In theory, the heat circulates through the hollow walls and heat shafts, entering the cells through iron grilles let into the walls. The upper cells are often comfortably warm while the lower ones remain unaffected. Periodically the Engineer Officer remembers to clean out the gap between the walls, and for this purpose chains are dropped from openings in the roof. In most prisons, however, the open-fire type of heating has been replaced by somewhat more up-to-date boiler arrangements. (See *stokehole; boiler-house.*) Heat is either conveyed to the existing hollow walls and shafts by steam-pipes, or hot-water pipes run the length of the cell blocks. In the latter case the pipes pass through each cell wall on the window side and the end cells have the benefit of one side being provided with extra piping which goes across the end of the block and back along the cells on the opposite side. Leaders and 'specials' are generally allotted these cells. In some prisons work in the shops has to stop if there is an electricity cut in winter, the water-circulation pumps being electrically driven. A great deal of heat is often lost through the bad layout of the old prisons and through cracked and broken fabric of some of the newer ones. Long pipelines are often essential. Electric heating is unheard of, but in the old gas-lighted prisons a great deal of warmth is gained from the jets and old lags often speak of the warmth of the cells in the days when they were lighted solely by gas-jets.

heaven (R). The top landing in a cell block or hall. See *landing.*

heavy. Anything 'heavy' refers only to anything very valuable or very bulky. A haul of furs, cloth, etc., from warehouse or shop. Any big jewel robbery. Warehouse-breakers are referred to as the 'heavy mob'.

heavy mob. Any gang that specialises in warehouse-breaking. Gangs which go in for big-scale robberies. (Particularly the former.)

heavy stuff. Motorised police who follow up a raid on club or 'gaff'. Reinforcements to a police raid, often using the Black Maria for transport. See *follow-up wagon; Black Maria; Sweeney.*

herbs. The coming of summer is greeted in the Old Bailey by a presentation of posies of cottage flowers to judges and aldermen. The court is also strewn with sweet-smelling herbs. This custom dates from 1750, when the Lord Mayor, an alderman, two judges, and several jurymen died from jail-fever, caught from the insanitary cells.

Smoking mixtures. When the 1947 increased tax on tobacco upset the weekly mite, one or two prison Governors experimented with herbal smoking mixtures, bought from herbalists and sold cheaply to the prisoners. On the whole the experiment was not a success; most of the mixtures were too hot to smoke and although mixed with ordinary tobacco they helped out the week's smoking, the initial enthusiasm did not last. Pipe smokers were able to hold out longer than cigarette smokers. Furthermore, in a number of prisons other substitutes were available. See *tobacco substitutes.*

hessian. Hessian is used extensively in the mailbag shops for postal and parcel mailbags and for those destined for hot climates, where they are usually burnt after use. Canvas is used for a better type of bag. See *mailbags; bagshop.*

Hi-Jack. For one gang to steal the haul which another has acquired. This saves the trouble of planning and breaking into premises. Since the opening of the Black Market this has become fairly common in England, but the expression 'Hi-Jack' is rarely used. It is another common Americanism introduced through 'thriller' fiction and gangster films.

H.M.P. His Majesty's Prison.

H.M.P. His Majesty's Pleasure. An indefinite sentence generally passed when there is doubt as to the defendant's sanity or on young offenders when faced with the capital charge. 'H.M.P.' is the same thing as being 'detained during the King's pleasure'.

H.O. Home Office.

hobbies. In some form or other hobbies have long been allowed in H.M. Prisons. Many years ago even Dartmoor convicts had their 'hobbies hour', when they were allowed to sit in the doorway of their cells, with an officer in charge to see that they did not talk to one another. In the 'modern prison' hobbies are greatly encouraged and among some of those indulged in are: aeromodelling—one man made a powered model which he was allowed to take out on discharge—rugmaking, weaving, knitting (occupational therapy), pottery, leatherwork, painting, and drawing. Carpentry is extremely popular and a high standard of workmanship is often reached. The tailoring shops generally help with a soft toy and leatherwork class after labour hours. Men are usually allowed to buy, at cost price, at least one toy made by themselves. Thus they are able to send birthday and Christmas presents to their children. Products of hobbies are sold at a small profit which goes towards a fund to purchase material and equipment. Near Christmas-time toys are made for distribution in local hospitals and children's homes. Unfortunately the American idea of a 'prison shop' is not allowed in this country, but the N.A.D.P.A.S. are trying to co-ordinate a system for centralising the output of hobbies classes, so that extra funds can be raised to help men on discharge. For this to be successful a high standard of production must be maintained in order to hold their own against competition. See *education*, etc.

hobo. Tramp. Americanism rarely heard in English prisons. See *chant; griddle; busker*, etc.

hoist. A female shoplifter. See *mystery*, etc.

holler wagon. The police radio car ('holler' = to shout). Also, *Sweeney*.

Hollesley Bay Colony. Borstal Institution with dormitory accommodation for 332. See *Borstal Institutions; Prisons*.

Holloway. The largest women's prison in the country, housed in an old-type building identical with the average man's prison. It accommodates both local prisoners and convicts and has a wing for Borstal girls whose licences have been revoked. There is also a hospital and maternity ward and a section reserved for women undergoing preventive detention (see *P.D.*). Cell accommodation is given as being about 644, with five rooms suitable for dormitories. There are also additional buildings in the grounds. See *women's prisons; Prisons; Borstal Institutions*.

Holy Joe. The prison chaplain (service slang). See *God Man*.

home-brew. Home-brewed wines, beer, and spirits have all been experimented with at some time or other in prison. The potato-still is the most popular and a crude rum can be made with burnt sugar and methylated spirits. A marrow, with the pips scraped out and filled with brown sugar, will also produce a potent drink. See *alcohol; beer*.

hoosegow. Another word used by youths who affect Americanisms. In the U.S.A. it refers to a police station.

hopped up. Under the influence of drugs. See *dope.*

hoppite. A lunatic. A 'nut'. An inmate of Broadmoor. (From the name of the Chief Medical Officer at Broadmoor, Dr. Hopwood.) See *certified*, etc.

hospital. Hospital quarters are attached to all prisons. Sometimes they consist only of a few specially reserved cells. A number of prisons, on the other hand, have well-equipped hospitals with clean wards, tiled bathrooms, dispensary, kitchen, etc. In certain cases men who are dangerously ill are sent out to the local hospital. Otherwise they are accommodated in Wormwood Scrubs, which has a well-fitted hospital with the best possible medical and surgical advice available. Women sisters attend in the wards and men from all prisons are sent there for surgical and other operations. It is also one of the most soulless parts of the prison system.

For X-ray examinations men are usually sent to a civilian hospital with an officer as escort. A number of the bigger hospitals of both local and convict prisons have their own X-ray units. See *psychiatric unit; bed, spring; sick; special sick; R.I.C.*, and below.

hospital cell. As part of the prison hospital there is a row of standard-size cells reserved for sick men who are not, for various reasons, accommodated in the wards. Except for a high-gloss paint, linoleum or similar floor-covering, these cells are identical with the ordinary block cell. There is an additional door or barred gate which can be locked while the door is left open. It is thus easy to watch the occupant. One of the most depressing sights in prison is to see a sick man confined to one of these cells for weeks on end. See *hospital*, etc.; *T.B. cells; V.D. cells; itch pitch.*

Hospital Officer. This is a rank in the uniformed branch of the Prison Service. To qualify it is necessary to pass an examination, usually held at a London prison, etc., and to be able to read, write, and to make up certain prescriptions. The Hospital Officer accompanies the Medical Officer on his daily round of the prison when he visits those men who have reported 'sick'.

hospital orderly. A leader or 'redband' is usually in charge of cleaning the wards, cells, corridors, and bathroom. If the hospital is a big one he may have cleaners under his charge. See *leader; redband.*

hospital visit. A man may have visitors in hospital if he is too sick to meet them in the rooms usually provided. See *visits; escort,* etc.

hot. Anything that has been stolen is spoken of as being 'hot'. A 'hot drag' = a stolen car, etc. See *hot stuff.*

hot district. See *morguey manor.*

hot stuff. Stolen property that is liable to be traced with comparative ease. See *hot; fence; swordsman,* etc.

hot water. Hot water is available only to those men who have been given Medical Officer's permission, which is not easily obtainable. It is very rare to find a hot-water tap in a prison block and men entitled to this commodity usually obtain it from the hall leader, who heats up a kettle on his gas ring. Otherwise it may have to be fetched from a dining-hall or from the hot tap located outside either the bathhouse or boilerhouse. Five minutes or so before the end of a working period orderlies are sent for a bucket of hot water from this tap so that men may wash their hands before leaving the shops. See *shaving; ablutions,* etc.

housebreaking. Housebreaking differs from burglary in that it can be committed only outside the hours of 9 p.m. and 6 a.m., and whereas burglary refers only to a private dwelling, housebreaking applies to any other building. See also *burglary.*

housemaster. A member of the non-uniformed branch of the Prison Service who takes charge of a house or hall. The men in that hall come to him for advice and with their various requests. As in a school, he is responsible for the welfare of the men under his care. A system introduced into the prisons from the Borstal Institutions. In 1947 the actual rank of 'Housemaster' was changed to that of Assistant Governor (Governor, 5th Class), though the duties and emoluments remained the same. In seniority an Assistant Governor ranks next to the Deputy Governor. The introduction of this rank, whose recruits are, fortunately, from the officer class of the services, has been the cause of a considerable amount of jealousy from the senior members of the uniformed staff. The wide gulf between these two, uniformed and non-uniformed members of the service, is lessening but is still wide. A newcomer, as Assistant Governor, is immediately up against a certain amount of opposition from the prison officers and their immediate superiors who resent the fact that, through no fault of their own, they are unqualified to hold office in a new system that aims, not at locking and unlocking doors but in moulding human character. See *Assistant Governor*, etc.

Howard, John. Born in 1728, John Howard is perhaps the best known among English prison reformers. While on his way to help the survivors of the Lisbon earthquake he was captured by a French privateer and imprisoned. Returning to England on parole, he negotiated his exchange and subsequently developed a keen interest in prisoners and prisons. He then toured European prisons and later those of England. While Acting Sheriff of Bedfordshire he became actively interested in prisons and brought about his well-known reforms. In common with other reformers and obsessionists he brought about a great deal of good at the expense of his own family and drove his son to the lunatic asylum. Most of our present-day prison buildings were built to his ideas, which included the conviction that solitary confinement, with only a Bible to read, was the best treatment during the first part of a man's sentence. By the standards of his day his reforms were indeed far-reaching. He died in about 1790.

Howard League. The most important of those societies whose aim is to improve the lot of the prisoner and to bring about reforms in our legal and penal systems. The League, named after the eighteenth-century reformer, is well supported by people of good standing and has done a great deal towards making prison more humane and comfortable without 'spoiling' the prisoner. It was through the offices of this League that, in pre-war days, men were able to earn up to one ounce of tobacco a week, and thus have an incentive for doing a good day's work. It seems to be the policy of the authorities to encourage such Leagues and Societies by giving them some sort of semi-official status. By doing this it is possible to prevent them from becoming too powerful and to suppress anything that would not make good public reading. See *N.A.D.P.A.S.*, *visitors; education; snout*.

H.S., the. The Home Secretary.

hulks, the. The old men-of-war formerly used as prisons. Some of these are still visible to-day, rotting by the banks of the River Thames.

hurry-up wagon. The Black Maria. See *follow-up wagon; heavy stuff; Black Maria*, etc.

I

ice. Diamonds. This word has completely supplanted the old word 'rocks'. See *schnide; jar.*

'imp.' Imprisonment. A man gets 'imp' as distinct from a 'lagging'. Any sentence of less than three years was 'imprisonment', longer than three years 'penal servitude'. With the abolition of penal servitude all sentences will be 'imprisonment' but with some distinction between 'long' and 'short' sentences which will determine the type of prison to which a man is to be sent. See *time; P.S.; Criminal Justice Act,* 1948.

Imperial Training College. A staff training college run at Wakefield Prison. Here all ranks entering the Prison Service receive their preliminary instruction. New officers, after a brief period in a suitable prison, are sent to the college. If they pass the tests there they are accepted as regulars and in due course are posted to one of the prisons.

Sir Alexander Paterson (*q.v.*) is credited with the instigation of the staff training college, which marks his conviction that the proper selection and training of prison staff is of paramount importance.

in the peek. In the observation cell; under observation. When a man 'smashes up' or loses his nerve he is usually placed in one of these cells. See *observation; observation cell.*

incinerator. Every prison has an incinerator for burning rubbish. The man in charge of this is usually a *redband* (*q.v.*) and is also responsible for cleaning the yards. It is a coveted job, as it allows a man to work entirely on his own, with considerable freedom of movement.

indicator. A metal indicator bearing the cell number is outside each door. When the bell is rung this metal bar drops and the landing officer can see at a glance which cell has rung. The indicator is also used by officers, when men are out at classes, etc., to show which cells are unoccupied. When men are locked in the indicator is pushed up, but if a man goes out it is pulled down. See *cell bell*.

indoor games. When summer has gone and it is no longer possible to allow men out in the yards or fields during association time, indoor games are organised. During 'term' time those prisons where classes are a speciality limit all games to a short period after 'supper'. During the recess extra association time is allowed and teams for darts, table tennis, draughts, chess, etc., are allowed to move from hall to hall under the same control system as that used for checking classes. Small prizes (tobacco) are sometimes given for inter-hall competitions but, as with outdoor games, the standard of sportsmanship is low. See *amusements; classes; education*, etc.

'inside.' The fact that one is in prison. Anyone serving a sentence is 'inside', as distinct from being 'outside' or free.

'inside.' The cry used by some officers when ordering men to their cells: 'Inside and bang your doors.' The men having 'banged' their doors are locked in automatically and the bolts, if fitted, are shot when the officer goes on his rounds at check-up time. See *All away*.

inspection, Medical Officer's. All receptions, discharges, and transfers are first seen by the prison doctor. Convicts are called up periodically, about every six months, and, with the abolition of penal servitude, it is assumed that 'long'-term men will be treated in the same way. See *reception; hospital; M.O.*, etc.

instructor. Although there are uniformed officers who qualify as instructors—as distinct from disciplinary and tradesmen officers—a large number of civilian instructors are employed by the Prison Service. See *civilian instructor; vocational training; prison officer.*

iron. One more Americanism used only by those who affect an American way of speech. Also, 'shooting iron'. See *heater; Roscoe.*

iron, half. Half-iron, bisexual. Homosexually inclined. One who, while not being a true homosexual, associates with people who are. See *pouff.*

iron hoof. Rhyming slang for *pouff.*

isolation cells. Those cells reserved for cases of infectious or contagious diseases. See *T.B. cells; V.D. cells; T.B. library; itch pitch,* etc.

itch pitch. Cells reserved for cases of scabies. See *isolation cells; fumigator.*

J

jane. A girl or woman. See *tart.*

jar. Faked diamonds. 'Phoney' diamonds = Schnide jars (from jam jar—glass). See *ice; snide* or *schnide.*

jelly. Gelignite. Used by the best *petermen* (*q.v.*) for blowing safes. The safe to be blown must be smothered with carpets, rugs, curtains, etc., and the right amount of gelignite neatly gauged if an accident is to be avoided. See *stripping; burning.*

jemmy. Popular instrument for forcing doors, lids, drawers, etc. Also, *stick; cane.*

Jew. All Jews are given every facility to follow their religious beliefs. A visiting rabbi comes to all prisons where there is a Jew and, if there is not a separate synagogue, there is at least a room set apart for them. When the occasion demands it, such as at Passover, they are allowed to have special food sent in by their friends or relations and it is prepared for them in the kitchen by one of their own faith. The Jewish cook is one of the men in prison with whom it is worth while to be on good terms. See *chapel; religion; baron*, etc.

jig-saw puzzles. Jig-saw puzzles have for long been one of the amusements permitted to certain prisoners. See *amusements*.

Jimmy Hix. American dope slang. See *dope*.

jockey. Early English thieves' cant (such as doxy, cove, gaff, etc.), which is occasionally used to-day, particularly by gipsies and 'didikais'. 'Hullo, Jockey, how are you?'

joey. Illegal parcel sent into—or out of—prison. See *stiff; trafficking*.

Johns. The police. 'Eye eye for the Johns' = look out for the police. Not in very common use. Probably derives from Robert Peel (see *copper*), which name the Cockney would delight in changing to John Peel.

Johnson. A *ponce* (*q.v.*). Probably from old English, as the word is found in seventeenth-century literature with the same meaning.

jougs (O). The iron neck ring of the old Scots pillory, which originates from 'jugum'.

Judas. The hole in the prison door through which a patrolling officer can keep watch on the occupant. Also, *peep*, etc.

judy (M). A girl. The more popular word to-day is *tart* (*q.v.*).

jug. Once-popular term for prison. Probably derives from the Latin 'jugum', a yoke, or from jougs.

jump. To steal. 'He jumped a drag' = he stole a car (or lorry). See *whizz; buzz, to*.

K

karvie. (Also, *carvie*.) Detective or police constable. See *bogey; dick; flattie; copper*, etc.

karzy. (Or *khazi*, probably from Hindustani.) Lavatory. 'He's gone to the karzy.' See *slash*.

karzy cleaner. The redband detailed to keep the yards tidy. He is also responsible for the cleanliness of the outside lavatories. See *yard redband*.

karzy paper. Lavatory paper. See *toilet paper*.

Kentucky hope (R). Lice, bugs, etc. See *dicks; cimex lectularius; big game*.

kettle. Gold watch. 'Kettle and piece' = watch and chain, usually referred to as 'the lot'. See *lot, the*.

keys. All cell and pass keys are kept in a special cupboard at the gate. The Governor, Deputy, Chief Officer, etc., have their own keys; other officers take the bunches given them. Each bunch is tagged with a number and must be handed to the Gate Officer before leaving the prison. Even the Governor must hand in his keys before leaving. Needless to say, no prisoner is (officially) ever allowed to touch an officer's keys and the most rigid precautions are taken with them. They must be attached to a chain buttoned to the belt and should any prisoner be discovered with a home-made key all locks in the prison are changed. This is no small matter, even in a local prison where there are probably some 300 or more locks. Gate keys are held only by the officer in charge of the main gate and no other key will unlock these. Pass keys are carried by senior officers or the Orderly Officers and when a lock is put on the 'double' it can be opened only by an officer in possession of a pass key.

It is only within recent years that officers have carried keys. In the 'old days' all officers, then called warders, lined up before the cells were unlocked and keys were issued by the Principal Officer. Each key bore a number and was carried on a huge circular ring. The officers were obliged to line up according to the number on their key and, having unlocked the cells, the key was returned to the ring in the same order. This ring is the origin of the still popular ring carried by the caricatured prison warder. See *gate screw*, etc.

ki (M). Cocoa or prison chocolate. See *cocoa*.

kick. See *putting in the leather*.

kike. See *Jew*.

King's Pleasure, the. See *H.M.P.*

Kingston. Borstal establishment for men whose licences have been revoked. Situated near Portsmouth, it was re-opened in 1948 after having been in use as a detention barracks. See *Prisons; Borstal Institutions*.

kip-house. See *doss-house; flophouse*.

kip, to. To sleep. 'To have a kip' = to have a nap. Also, *doss; flophouse*.

kitbags. Kitbags for use of the police and men of the services are a product of prison bagshops. They are made on the prison sewing-machines, which may be either hand or power operated. See *mailbags; bagshop*, etc.

kite man. A forger (rhyming slang, write—kite). A cheque is sometimes called a *kite*. Also, *pen man*.

knitting. Knitting has been encouraged in a number of prisons, where it is carried out either as a class of a dozen men or so, or in some cases as an individual occupation to be done in the privacy of the cell. See *hobbies; education.*

knock. To cheat or to 'con'. 'He knocked the new man for a nicker' = he cheated the new man out of a pound. See *con.*

knock out, to. To burgle. To knock out a place or gaff, is to burgle it thoroughly, leaving it cleaned out of anything of any value. See *do; case*, etc.

L

labour. Prison term for work. 'Where is No. 99?'—'He is not yet back from labour.' Although the potential manpower available in prison has been realised, little has been done to turn it to full advantage. Even to-day the chief occupation is the monotonous sewing of mailbags, repairing of prison footwear, and numerous small tasks which have to be done. Prison shops produce all that is required in the prisons; cloth for clothing and bedding is woven at Wakefield; prison furniture is made in various carpenters' shops; and boots and shoes for officers and men are made in various prisons throughout the country. The quality of most prison-produced articles is not always equal to that found elsewhere, although, in all fairness, it must be admitted that a high degree of skill can be found in various branches of prison production.

The G.P.O. is probably the most important prison customer (see *mailbags*). Others include the Admiralty (fenders, hammocks, etc.), Ministry of Supply, Air Ministry, R.A.O.C., though a curtailment of contracts at the end of the war caused numerous problems in the prisons (see *cell tasks*). The principal prison shops include : tailors', where material from Wakefield is made into suits, shirts, etc. ; tinsmiths', who produce oil cans, sugar tins, etc., for prison and Post Office use ; carpenters', who make, not only furniture for cells and officers' quarters, but various other articles for use by various Government departments ; and, of course, the inevitable bagshop. Basketwork is also carried out in some prisons, under the supervision of instructors. So far as clothing is concerned, a great deal of underwear and socks were bought from surplus Army stores ; also shoes made for use in munition factories. These were of a superior quality to those produced in the prisons. See *clothing; shoes; P.W.S.; Mint, the Royal; tailors' shop; baskets.*

labour hours. Working hours. These vary according to the type of prison. In the 'bad' prisons, where shortage of staff and work make other arrangements difficult, the working day runs from about 9 a.m. to 11.30 a.m. and from 2 p.m. to 4.30 p.m., after which all men are locked in cells. In the better prisons the more normal hours run from 8 a.m. to 11.50 a.m. and from 1 p.m. to 4.50 p.m. Outside parties usually come in much later in the summer, when there is a great deal to be done, harvesting, etc., and in the winter they come in at dusk. See *time-table; farm parties.*

lag. Strictly speaking, a convict, *i.e.* one sentenced to penal servitude ; but occasionally the word is used when referring to one who has served several short sentences. 'Old lag', a recidivist. See *old lag; P.S.; Criminal Justice Act,* 1948.

lagging. Three years' penal servitude. See *time; Criminal Justice Act,* 1948; *P.S.*

lagging station. A convict prison where long-term men are sent. See *Prisons.*

lamps, emergency. In addition to gas-jets, still to be found in most prisons, candles and a very few electric torches (intended for the night watch only) are available in the case of an emergency. An order was given to restore the main gas-points in case of winter electricity cuts. See *candles; lighting.*

landing. Steel and stone galleries run round the upper cell blocks. Each tier is called a landing and there are generally from two to four landings to a block or wing. Some of the more modern prisons, of which we have only too few, follow the French plan with only two floors. See *landing officer; safety net; heaven.*

landing officer. The officer in charge of a particular landing in the block. Where possible one officer is detailed to each landing and this is always the rule at opening-up or locking-up time. Shortage of staff has made it necessary to limit the number of officers. Where men 'associate' in the halls, particularly the modern two-floor halls, one officer on the ground floor can usually manage to look after one hall. See *screw; hall; landing.*

landing screw. Landing officer.

languages. Owing to the variety of nationalities in British prisons one hears many different tongues spoken, although most foreign prisoners (nearly always seamen) speak English after a fashion.

Black men, brown men, yellow men, near-whites, and half-castes are all thrown in together with white men and it is only to be expected that fighting occurs through racial dislike, particularly in the London prisons and those near the big seaports. Although there is a certain amount of colour prejudice in prison it is safe to say that it appears less than that met with outside. Although most coloured men are Mohammedans or Buddhists and are allowed the food demanded by their beliefs, they have no facilities for special prayer or services. A greater hardship many coloured men suffer, particularly in convict prisons, is the lack of reading matter in their native language. The African or Indian serving a long sentence suffers doubly by these privations and often leads a lonely life through having no compatriot to 'chum up' with. See also *education*.

laundry. Nearly every prison has its own laundry, in which a small party of prisoners work under an officer. Some prisons do the laundry work for smaller ones or for the local police. The work turned out for outside bodies is on a very different level from that done for the prison. New garments are inevitably ruined after the first laundering and, until socks from ex-Army stores were issued, the prison socks were shrunk to fit only the smallest foot. For long this has been a cause of discontent among prisoners, who frequently complain to the already overworked Medical Officer.

Men working on the laundry parties have frequent opportunities for trading. They have their regular customers for ironed shirts, which are often specially bleached to remove the pin-stripe lines. Good socks, neatly pressed trousers, and the best underwear can always be obtained, for a consideration, from these men. See *buy; sell; snout; dhobying*.

lavatories. In local prisons where labour hours are short and men spend a great deal of time locked up in their cells they have no access to the lavatory recess. Lavatories are, however, provided in the workshops and in the exercise yards, but on the diet provided in prison regular habits are not easily acquired and considerable discomfort is experienced by the enforced confinement in cell with the crude arrangements at hand. In winter the freezing-up of the outside lavatories causes added discomfort. Even in the more up-to-date prisons lack of suitable sanitary arrangements makes the 'slop out' hour an experience of indescribable disgust for the newcomer, and the stench is something to which the average reasonable citizen (of which there are more than a few in prison) can never become accustomed.

As the only water-tap is usually situated above the slop sink some prisoners can never bring themselves to drink water, with the result that a healthy habit is denied them.

Pleasant to the eye of the visiting magistrate on his rounds is the spare water-tap provided in some prisons. This is at the entrance to the recess and is over a little drain which is neatly white-washed each day. The original intention was that it should be used for filling water-jugs, but in a number of prisons it is a punishable offence to touch this tap. See also *karzie*, etc.

law, the. See *'lor', the*.

layabout. Anyone who leads an idle life. One who never works and has plenty of time to take things easily. One on remand, though in this case the more usual word is *laydown*.

laydown. A man on remand; presumably so called because he is not obliged to work and has ample opportunity to sleep or to lie on his bed. In actual fact he is not allowed to use his bed until the official hour for 'beds down'. See *remand*.

leader. A privileged prisoner or convict. He wears a distinctive badge or armband and is allowed a considerable amount of freedom. He may walk about parts of the prison unaccompanied by an officer and he may take parties of up to about a dozen men from one

place to another. He is also allowed to stay up till
9 p.m. instead of being locked in at the usual hour of
8. A 'leader's room' is set aside for his recreation
and this is shared, in convict prisons, by the 'specials'.
The leader system is an outcome of what the old-time
warders called a 'trustie'. See *redband; stage; Special;
trustie.*

Leeds. Local prison, usually referred to as Armley Gaol,
with cell accommodation for 477 in cells.

leggner (R). Sometimes used instead of 'stretch' when
referring to one year's imprisonment. See *time; stretch,*
etc.

Leicester. Local prison with cell accommodation for
203. Owing to shortage of accommodation the dormitory system was started here as long ago as 1945
and the library redband was placed in charge of about
12 men. It is also a 'topping' prison. See *Prisons.*

Lemon and Balkan States. An example of rhyming
slang popular with a certain type of prisoner. Trans-
lated it means 'wash and grease' up, greasing the hair
being an important part of the 'spiv's' toilet. (Greece—
grease. Lemon squash being the rhyming slang for
wash.)

letters. Prison rules allow a man to write and to receive
one letter a month. A prisoner who has not written a
letter 'out' cannot receive a letter from friend or
relation. People outside may only write in reply to a
letter received from a prisoner. That is the ruling
according to orders, but it is varied in many ways,
particularly in the training establishments, where, for
example, a letter is allowed every three weeks and a
man may receive two or even three letters 'in'. A
leader has the additional privilege of having a letter
a fortnight on which to write out (see *applications,*

Governor's). Extra letters are granted if good reasons are given when asking for them, and the Chaplain also has the power to issue 'special letters' which do not go through the normal censor channels. If a man has no one to write to he may not give his letters away, but if, on the other hand, he cannot have visits he may have a letter in place of a visit. See *visits*.

The official letters are stamped at public expense, but should a man wish to write an airmail letter or a letter to a foreign country he may pay for it out of his money in 'property', on making formal application to the Governor. In the more modern prisons such requests are handled by the Assistant Governor (see *House-master*). See *pens and ink; censor; Christmas letter; reception letter; visits*.

Lewes. Local prison, accommodating 289 in cells. See *Prisons*.

Ley Hill. 'Star' convict prison. The first of its kind, Ley Hill (formerly known as Tortworth) is an 'open-camp' prison and is situated near Bristol in what was, during the war, an American Army V.D. hospital. In 1946, when Camp Hill reverted to a Borstal Institution, a small party of men went in advance to Tortworth to prepare this for the use of convicts. Other parties followed and the shops were moved down there. In October the main body of men was moved in motor-coaches and, with one or two long-term convicts about to be released, Camp Hill remained empty and ready for the first 'boys'. See *Prisons; Camp Hill*.

library. Every prison has a library of some sort. Officially there is an allowance from the Home Office for the purchase of books other than devotional, reference, and technical. This was 1s. 3d. per head until 1945, when it was raised to 2s. per head. In many prisons the distribution of books is simple. An officer, detailed to be in charge of the library for that week, goes round the prison one day a week. The library redband and a cleaner accompany him with one or two laundry baskets filled with books. First they collect all books from the cells, and in their place throw in whatever books come to hand from the filled basket. The number and type of books allowed weekly vary from prison to prison and according to the 'stage' a prisoner has reached. An average allowance might be two 'devotional' books and one fiction. There is no limit to the number of textbooks allowed, providing the authorities are satisfied that the man is studying. It is comparatively simple to satisfy the library officer in most prisons.

Men may have books sent in, but 'after a reasonable period'—which is interpreted in various ways—they must be handed over to the library. In this way the bigger prisons are able to build up quite good libraries. Unfortunately the great majority of prisoners are satisfied with the 'blood and thunder' type of pulp literature and good books go unread. There is a system whereby prisons interchange their library books, but the best books do not, as a rule, leave the prison where they first entered.

The 'modern' prisons have whole-time library officers, an educated leader to help him, and a number of suitable redbands. The library is looked on as an important part of the prison system and men are helped to get the books they want to read. In some prisons they are allowed to go to the library on fixed days and there pick their week's reading. Technical and educational books are generally kept by the Education Office for the benefit of the men who really wish to learn something while serving their time.

Library books can always be 'bought'. That is, the man who has the 'money'—tobacco—can always get the books he wants and without waiting. Where a prison has a block for 'remands' the library staff are able to obtain extra tobacco because the 'remands' are allowed to buy their own. Moving freely about the prison, the library leader is in an admirable position to assist in the ever-current movement of tobacco and pound notes. See *education; periodicals; snout.*

library leader. Prisoner appointed to assist the library officer and to supervise the redbands.

library officer. A whole-time library officer is appointed in the more up-to-date prisons.

licence. Once known as 'ticket of leave', the convict's licence has now been abolished by the Criminal Justice Act of 1948, the relevant clause of which came into effect early in 1949. Until this date the convict could earn the same remission as the prisoner—one-third of his sentence. Whereas the prisoner was then free to go his way, the convict was limited by the provisions of his licence and was obliged to report once a month to the police unless specifically excused this onerous duty.

Abolition of the licence was opposed by the police, whose duty it is to keep an eye on all suspicious characters. The chief grievance of the rearrested convict was that, having once served a sentence, it was virtually impossible for him to go 'straight'. He could take no employment without his employer being informed of his past and on the least pretext he could be taken to the police station for questioning. On licence he was restricted in many ways; he was not allowed to stand in bus queues or to stay out after ten o'clock; he could not change his address or town without notifying the police. Undoubtedly there are many men who ought always to be under some sort of supervision, but these were the types who managed to escape from the conditions of their 'tickets', whereas the honest man, with every good intention, tried to

stick rigidly to the rules and provisions, which were
the cause of his eventually getting into trouble again.

For those whose conduct requires it, a modified
system of reporting has been devised and a great deal
of this will be handled by the probation officers.

Lifebuoy. See *bath orderly.*

lifer. One serving a sentence of life imprisonment. A
man serving a sentence of imprisonment or penal servitude is usually free to go out of prison on licence
after serving two-thirds of his time (see *remission*), but
a 'lifer' may serve anything from a year or so up to
about fifteen years. This depends on his behaviour and
on the Medical Officer's report. To-day a life sentence,
for a reprieved murderer, for example, means about
seven to eight years (see *murderers*).

light of love. Rhyming slang for the Prison Governor.
See *Guv; dep; screwdriver.*

lighting. Electricity has replaced gas in nearly all the
English prisons (see *gas*, etc.). As the original gas-jet
for cell lighting was located by the door, it followed
that when electricity was installed the first lamps
should be placed in the same glass-fronted niche. Later
they were wired to the ceiling, about a foot inside the
cell door, and the gas-niche was bricked in. Now the
cell lamp, generally about 25 watts, though increased
to 40 watts in some prisons, is in process of being
moved to the centre of the ceiling, which in many
ways is a better position, though a difficult one for
the man who reads in bed. See *voltage*, etc.

lights out. All cell lights are turned off at 9 o'clock by
the landing cleaners (who are, in some prisons, allowed
up late for this purpose), or by the hall leader or redband. Only men who have special permission, and

leaders, specials, and men on correspondence courses are allowed the extra hour of light.

In the morning the lights are switched on between 6 and 6.15 a.m. to allow men to dress and tidy their cells before unlocking time. See *'All away'; lighting; night screw.*

lime. Lime is still used at the burial of some executed prisoners and for this purpose is listed in the stores books. It has been found, however, that in some soils it has preserved the bodies, and consequently hanged men are sometimes buried in boxes filled with charcoal and perforated to allow a maximum of moisture to penetrate. See *executions.*

Lincoln. Local prison, accommodation 393. See *Prisons.*

listed. Certified insane. See *hoppite.*

literary efforts. No prisoner is allowed, according to the instructions in official exercise books, to take out any '(i) notes in shorthand or cypher, (ii) any original composition in prose, verse, or music, (iii) any design, drawing, or painting, other than geometrical, mechanical, or scientific drawings made in connection with an approved educational course'.

On numerous occasions the question has been broached, 'Why may a prisoner not write stories or verse, or draw or paint for publication?' During the debate on the Criminal Justice Bill of 1948 this question was dealt with in light and sarcastic vein with references to potential John Bunyans. Mr. Chuter Ede, reported in a national newspaper, replied that men were now allowed writing facilities and that the question did not now arise. It is quite true that exercise books are easily obtainable and pencils are issued, but the rule of writing for publication still stands and the above-quoted order is still being printed in exercise books for issue to prisoners.

Liverpool. Local prison with cell accommodation for 705 men.

loaded. A man is 'loaded' when he has plenty of anything. A 'snout baron' is loaded when he has just got in his stock of tobacco. A prisoner sees another with a full tobacco tin; he remarks, 'Cor, you ain't arf loaded.' Plenty of any commodity. 'Loaded with sugar (buns, 'butter', etc.). See *snout; baron.*

loaf. Head. 'To use one's loaf' = to think. See also *nutting.*

lob. Pay. The weekly pay received by prisoners. 'Gash lob' = spare money. (See *pay; gash.*) Also, to throw. 'Lob it over' = throw it.

lob. Ear. See also *tab.*

'local.' A local, as distinct from a convict prison or training centre, etc. A county prison. See *nick; Prisons.*

lock up. The final check-up by the day officers is carried out before 9 p.m., when the last prisoners are locked up. The night staff then take over and recheck. This latter check is disturbing where men have their lights out by 8 p.m. The night officer invariably switches the light on and off to make quite sure the occupant is in his cell. See *lights out; night screw,* etc.

lodger. A prisoner in transit who spends a night at a prison on his route. See *escort,* etc.

'loid or **Lloyd.** Celluloid. Used for opening doors with Yale or Yale-type locks. Shaped like an oval, the narrow end, which has been shaved thin, is inserted at the bottom of the door to be forced. The bottom is always easier to force open a fraction of an inch. Gripping the 'loid with both hands the operator works it upwards and under the lock, which slides back automatically. If the snib is down, of course, a 'loid is useless, but for unoccupied premises it is adequate.

The 'loid is easily carried inside the hatband. It is an offence to carry one, as it comes under the list of 'H.B.I.' or house-breaking implements. The word originates from rhyming slang, Harold Lloyd—a once well-known comedian—celluloid. See *H.B.I.*

lolly. Policeman (from the rhyming slang, lollypop—cop). See *bogey; dick*, etc.

loop the loop. Rhyming slang for soup.

'lor', the. The law. The police. A policeman. Any executive of the law.

lot, the. Watch and chain together. See also *kettle*.

love letters. A certain type of prisoner is unable to refrain from writing letters to the friend of his choice. Writers of love letters can be divided into two categories, the man who has opportunities to meet women, and the out-and-out homosexual. In some local prisons both men and women are housed and though they are segregated and supervised with the utmost care they somehow or other contrive to carry on some sort of affair by writing the most passionate letters to each other. The homosexual does the same thing—letters are written on scraps of toilet paper, rolled into a tiny ball and flicked into the cell of another. This type of person even exchanges letters during labour or association hours when there is every opportunity for talking. See *pouff; swinging the line*.

Lowdham Grange. Borstal Institution with dormitory accommodation for 204. See *Prisons; Borstal Institutions*.

lug. Ear. See *tab*.

lumber. A garage. Store-place for stolen goods. 'A hot drag in the lumber' = a stolen car in the garage. See *drum; gaff*, etc.

M

Maidstone. Training centre with cell accommodation for about 350 and a number of dormitories. Celia Fiennes, in her diary of her ride through England, mentions Maidstone as having a 'large gaol'. In its present site the prison has housed 'local' prisoners of both sexes, as well as convicts. At the beginning of World War II the convicts were moved to Camp Hill (*q.v.*) and, with the exception of a wing reserved for remands and very short-term men, the prison became a training centre. In 1944 it was established as the training centre for the S.E. Region, including London, and in 1946, Canterbury Prison being returned by the Navy, all remands and 'local' men were moved there from Maidstone.

Maidstone had started by following the Wakefield system. Quickly it moved ahead of the Yorkshire prison and is to-day undoubtedly the most progressive in the country. The methods may be unorthodox but the results are promising. Not all men sent there are 'stars'; many have bad records and, through the non-existence of a proper selection board, many of the very worst types find themselves in surroundings which they cannot appreciate. There is always the type that take kindness and trust for signs of weakness. After being given every chance such men, if they do not then respond, are returned.

The statistical results for Maidstone will not be available for some years, so a comparison with Wakefield, on the same basis, is not yet possible. That the Maidstone system does work is shown, among other things, by the letters and messages received by the Governor from 'old boys'.

Prisoners at Maidstone carry out the normal working

5*

duties of prison life. All printing for the Prison Service is done there and there is also a large carpenters' shop, a tailors' shop, and a bagshop. In the latter a variety of work is carried on, from the dismantling of aircraft gun-turrets, for metal salvage, to the stapling of note-books for the Metropolitan Police.

Three whole-time vocational courses are run (see *vocational training*) and there is also a large farm party (*q.v.*). Men from Maidstone are selected to fill the camp at Aldington (*q.v.*).

Amusements are plentiful and include whist and bridge (see *amusements; cards*). All *hobbies* (*q.v.*) are encouraged and the hobbies classes are always full.

The educational programme is the Governor's chief interest and he has the support of over forty voluntary teachers and lecturers, who take a variety of classes and some ten discussion groups. Attendance is volun-tary, though all men are expected to attend at least once a week. The average attendance nightly is about 200 out of some 350 men. In addition there are nearly one hundred men on correspondence courses (*q.v.*). Prisoners also take classes and the Kent Education Committee co-operate to the full in helping with teachers for special subjects, lecturers, etc.

Subjects for one term (Autumn 1948) were as follows:

Discussions: General Knowledge, for the semi-illiterate; six on Current Affairs; 'This Week in Par-liament'; Sociology; 'Farming and Stockbreeding'; Play Reading (2); 'The British Commonwealth'; 'Church and Society'; Sports and Quizzes.

Debate: Friday night is reserved for the Debating Group, which numbers about 130 men. Visitors join in and subjects are selected by a small committee of prisoners and the Education Office staff.

Classes: Acting; Art (oil and water-colour); Com-mercial Art (Advertising, etc.); Auto-Engineering;

Book-keeping; Carpentry; Diesel Engines; Electricity
(one elementary and one advanced); First Aid; French;
Gardening; German; Hairdressing (by the prison
barber); Harmony and Music Theory; Horticulture;
Knitting (occupational therapy); Leatherwork; three
classes for various stages of progress in Mathematics
(two are taken by civilians and one by the Engineering
Instructor); Pewter Work; P.T.; Radio Hobbies;
Rugmaking; Shorthand; Spanish; Tailoring, theory
and practice (also soft toy making in the tailoring
shop); Weaving; Woodwork machining.

With such a programme there is every opportunity
for a man to make full use of his time while serving
a sentence. Numerous foreign visitors are shown over
Maidstone, which they may compare with their own
systems in their various countries. Representatives
from the Scottish prisons have studied the system and
are applying it to a similar establishment in Scotland.
See *W.E.A.*

mailbags. For many years the principal occupation of
the prisoner has been the making of mailbags, which
has placed the G.P.O. in the lead of prison customers.
Machines are rarely used and the hand-sewing is a
constant grouse with prisoners. With the cancellation
of wartime contracts a general 'go slow' production
had to be followed and it was quite common to unsew
perfectly good mailbags so that they could provide
more work by being resewn.

Bags are of three kinds, a cheap hessian, a better
quality canvas bag, and the large parcel-post bags.
The operation in the making of a bag is simple. The
material is cut to the required sizes on the cutting table,
folded, and distributed to those who sew up the sides
and bottoms; each bag is then turned and double-
sewn. Next, stiffener ropes—odd lengths of coir rope
being used—are sewn round the mouths, and finally

the 'tabs' (*q.v.*) holding the metal rings are sewn on. After stencilling (*q.v.*) the bags are sent to the manufacturing stores (*q.v.*) for despatch.

The official figures (from the Report of the Commissioners, 1945, published in 1947) show that between 1939 and 1944 a total of 10,171,471 mailbags were produced, and in 1945 alone the number was 2,410,000. In addition nearly 4,000,000 old mailbags were repaired. With up-to-date machinery and freedom to compete in the open market the prison workshops could make our prisons self-supporting. See *labour; tab; stencils; wax; suicide*, etc.

'mailbags.' Name given to those prison workshops devoted to the production of mailbags and other articles using hessian, canvas, and rope. Here are made such things as kitbags, ships' fenders, coaling sacks, hammocks, mattresses, pillows, slippers, and anything which can be sewn by hand or machine. Other work includes small soldering jobs for the G.P.O. and the dismantling of parts for salvage.

Manchester. Local prison for men and women, with accommodation for 976. See *Prisons*.

manor. A district. 'What manor do you perform in?' = in what district do you operate (or live)? See *morguey manor; cut*, etc.

manslaughter. The suggestion that murder should be divided into degrees of guilt was rejected when the Criminal Justice Bill came up in 1948. Although we have not this system the actual working of our law brings about a somewhat similar result. Murder in England can be reduced to manslaughter and sentence passed accordingly, but where guilt of murder is proved there is only one sentence which can be passed; that is, sentence of death (see *death sentence*). Again, however, this can be commuted to a sentence of life imprisonment. See *murderers; H.M.P.; lifer; time.*

manufacturing stores. Prison stores where all material is handed out to the various production shops and where the finished articles are packed for despatch. See *production.*

'mark his card.' Warning a friend that someone is about to betray him or 'do him up'. 'A' marks 'B's' card when he tells 'C' that 'B' is planning to do him, 'C', an injury. A tip-off.

Mary Warner. Marijuana. See *dope.*

mats. Floor mats of the 'coconut' type are made in some local prisons, also door mats for Government departments. Being a messy and dusty operation they are made only in the shops and cannot be made in cells. They also need special frames which would be too cumbersome to move about. See *bagshop; mailbags; carpet.*

mats, cell. A strip of coconut matting is provided for each cell. On Sundays at exercise time these are taken out into the yards for a beating. Inspecting officers always lift these mats and if the floor underneath is found to be dirty a chalked message is left—'Scrub'. See *cell; furniture, cell,* etc.

mattresses. These are made in the prison bagshops and are stuffed with coir. Those intended for the use of officers are stuffed with flock. See *mailbags; bagshop; coir.*

meat pie. Pasty issued with some meals. Any 'pie', meat, bacon, or vegetable, issued at dinner time. See *menu; 'who dunnit?'*

medicine. At least one prison Hospital Officer is a qualified dispenser. When prisoners who are not sick enough to go to hospital are ordered medicine by the Medical Officer it is left in their cells by the Hospital Officer, who does a daily round of the blocks for this purpose. He is accompanied by a cleaner from the hospital, who carries the bottles and 'tots' on a tray in front of him; rather like the tray used for selling cigarettes and chocolates in cinemas in pre-war days. There are a number of standard medicines which are doled out automatically: white powder for stomach complaints; zinc ointment for abrasions; linctus for colds, etc. See *hospital; tot.*

menu. Instructions from the Home Office lay down the exact amounts of foodstuffs to which a man is entitled. The prison Medical Officer inspects the food each day, eating a meal on a table laid for him, with the food taken from that which is to be issued to the men. The diet as ordered by the Home Office is balanced and arranged by the medical staff. Each week the Officer-cook submits a typed 'menu' to the Home Office, showing exactly what meals will be issued. Reading this menu is most encouraging. The following is a copy of a week's meals at a prison late in 1948:

Breakfast (daily): porridge, bread, butter, tea.

Midday:

Sunday: hot-pot, potatoes, cabbage, gravy, bread roll, tea.

Monday: meat and vegetable soup, potatoes, cabbage, bread roll.

Tuesday: meat pie, potatoes, cabbage, gravy, bread roll.

Wednesday: fried fish, potatoes, cabbage, semolina, bread roll.

Thursday: vegetable soup, sausage pie, potatoes, cabbage, bread roll.

Friday: baked fish, potatoes, cabbage, semolina, bread.

Saturday: bacon pie, potatoes, cabbage, beans, bread.

Tea (daily): bread, butter, tea, plus extras as follows: Sunday, jam; Monday, cheese and beetroot; Tuesday, sausage rolls; Wednesday, jam; Thursday, apple-pie.

Supper (daily): cocoa.

Note: The fish is usually served fortnightly as fried fish, or when enough fat has been saved from the cocoa. Bread rolls were issued at dinner time instead of altering the standard size of the 'cob' when bread was removed from the list of rationed commodities. A cell instruction card (No. 118) advises men as follows: 'In most prisons no meal is served after 4.40 in the afternoon. If this is so in the prison where you are, you should keep part of the food issued to you at 4.40 to eat later on before going to bed.' Since this instruction cocoa is now issued at 8 p.m. (see *cocoa*). Before that a man could, if he wished, save half his 'cob' and margarine and half a pint of cocoa to drink cold before going to bed. See *cob; butter; yellow peril; 'who dunnit?'; depth-charge; duff* (not in the above menu, but when issued is described as *plumduff*); *U.S. Day*, etc.

messenger. Each day one officer is detailed to act as messenger. He may be called on to take a telegram to the Post Office, to collect a parcel, or to make some special purchases. See *prison officer.*

milk. Fresh milk is issued to T.B. prisoners and is allowed to men engaged in certain unhealthy tasks such as spray-painting, stereo-block making, etc. Otherwise it is only given on Medical Officer's authority. See *diet.*

milk diet. Special diet given to sick men on the Medical Officer's orders. This, outside hospital treatment proper, is generally given to those suffering from stomach disorders, a not infrequent trouble with newcomers. See *diet.*

135

'millionaires.' There are many men in prison who talk all the time of big money. They boast of their Rolls Royces, town and country houses, and of the luxurious style in which they are accustomed to live. Invariably such men actually own nothing and leave the prison wearing a D.P.A. suit (*q.v.*). Rarely do these people possess even the right manner to be convincing. Occasionally one meets an educated man who is also prone to megalomania, but all types eventually give themselves away. The Governor and staff soon get to know them and recognise the type on his arrival. The dream world in which such men live is convincing only to themselves, and particularly noticeable are the solicitors' clerks who pose as lawyers, medical orderlies and hospital attendants who pretend to be doctors, and the small trader who imagines himself as a big business tycoon.

milned in. Locked in. 'To miln' = to lock up. From the well-known makers of locks and safes. See *chubbed in; screw up.*

Mint, the Royal. The prisons make various articles on contract for the Royal Mint. These are mostly canvas moneybags. See *labour; production; mailbags.*

mirrors. A small mirror is part of the standard cell equipment. It is not allowed where a man is liable to attempt suicide. It provides a certain amount of amusement when the sun is shining. Occupants of cells in the opposite block can be entertained or annoyed by flashed rays. See *pastimes; tapped signals.*

miscellaneous stores. Those stores which issue foodstuffs, cleaning materials, and furniture, etc., to the prison. See *manufacturing stores; porter.*

mix it, to. To put one man against another. To make trouble. See *mark his card; grass, to.*

M.O. Medical Officer. Owing to the large number of men for whom he is responsible the M.O.'s task is not an easy one. Only the larger prisons have more than one resident doctor, a locum attending at others during the absence of the resident. Medical examinations are often cursory and unsatisfactory, but in spite of overwork there are prison doctors who take a genuine interest in many men's cases and who try to help individual men. See *psychiatric unit*.

Mohammedans. Are permitted special food and excused parade for chapel. See *religion*, etc.

monkey. Fifty pounds. See *pony; white*, etc.

moon, a. One month's imprisonment. See *time; woodener*.

Moor. the. Dartmoor Convict Prison.

moosh. 'Moosh' is used more as a greeting: 'Hullo, Moosh' (Romany). See also *tosh*.

morguey manor. A district dangerous for 'screwing' jobs. A well-policed district. See *manor*.

mortuary. In most prisons there is a separate mortuary for use in case of sudden death. Wherever possible a dangerously sick prisoner is removed to a local hospital, but occasionally a man dies, or is killed, in prison.

mouthpiece. Defence lawyer or counsel.

mug. See *steamer*.

muniment room. Prison archives. The record room. Here are found the musty volumes of past hangings, whippings, and the brief details of sentences of deportation passed on children for such trivial offences as stealing a loaf of bread. Many such volumes were unearthed during the war by officers detailed to clear out the muniment rooms to aid the paper salvage. It is said that works by Oscar Wilde were found at

Reading but, as no original work by a prisoner may go out of prison, they had to be destroyed (see *literary efforts*).

murderers. Men sentenced to death for murder are, in most cases, reprieved. Unless certified insane, when they go to Broadmoor (*q.v.*), the sentence is commuted to one of life imprisonment. In England murder is regarded as the gravest crime; worse than child rape or sadistic torturing. The wilful murderer, the man who plans a murder for financial gain, hangs. The majority of murders are killings which occur on the spur of the moment—crimes of passion, the drunken fight. In these cases the likelihood of a recurrence is negligible and, having no degrees of murder in England, the charge is usually reduced to manslaughter (*q.v.*).

Murderers in the convict prisons, the 'star' prisons at least, are for the most part likeable men. Contrary to popular opinion, there is nothing out of the ordinary about them. They are victims of unfortunate circumstances and they pay dearly. Recognising this the Home Office has, during the past decade or so, reduced the length of the average life sentence to round about eight years. Naturally, discharge depends entirely on medical opinion. Murderers have gone out after but a year or so. In one case, a mercy killing, the man was released within a year. Other men do not qualify for release; perhaps they develop violent tempers, become quarrelsome and mentally unstable. To release any murderer is a responsibility which rests with the Home Office. The Civil Service has a reputation for not taking chances, and the very fact that they consider releasing murderers after a few years speaks volumes for their understanding. See *executions; manslaughter; lifer; Special; psychiatric unit.*

mush faker. One who repairs umbrellas. An occupation of the 'diddikais' or near Romanies. See *diddikai*.

music. Classical music is not denied prisoners and the larger prisons run music appreciation classes, which are given by enthusiastic visitors or by prisoners who use borrowed records. Occasionally there is an officer who appreciates good music and he runs the class, bringing in the records and electric record player. See *education; radio.*

music practice. Men are allowed to play musical instruments in their cells at certain hours. These men are, for the most part, members of the prison band. The standard of playing is not always of the best and practice, unless of popular tunes on an accordion, provokes a certain amount of catcalling from men who wish to read.

mustard. Mustard is allowed in some dining-halls and is mixed by the hall leader, who is responsible for issuing it to the tables.

mystery. A stranger (female) to the district. 'A mystery in the manor' = a new girl in the locality. A 'mystery' is frequently used in the confidence game. It can also refer to a girl who is 'down and out' in London and looking for a job. See *manor; cut; con; creep, to.*

N

N.A.D.P.A.S. National Association of Discharged Prisoners' Aid Societies. More commonly known as the 'D.P.A.' (Discharged Prisoners Aid). See *D.P.A.*

'name and number.' When a man is marched in to see the Governor in his office the officer in charge of marshalling the men never fails to order, 'Stand to attention! Name and number to the Governor.' Years of habit are, no doubt, the cause of this parrot-like repetition. Good-natured officers, aware of it, some-times have difficulty in not smiling when they catch the eye of a prisoner who is well known to officers and Governor. See *applications*, etc.

N.A.P.V. National Association of Prison Visitors. This Association had its twenty-fifth anniversary on 2 May 1947. Its unincorporated history is much longer. On the women's side it traces a descent from the original Ladies' Committee formed in Newgate by Elizabeth Fry. Mr. Winston Churchill may also be awarded credit for encouraging the prison visitor, who brings to the prisoner a touch of the outside world.

These visitors are given a cell key at the gate and there they collect their visiting list. They enter a man's cell—springing the lock first (*q.v.*) and are free to chat without supervision. They may not bring in any of the prohibited articles. In the more modern prison (see *training centre; Wakefield; Maidstone*) their services are no longer required, though some still have their list of men to be visited. The visitors to these establishments are usually men and women who take classes or discussion groups, and where men spend most of the day in company with their fellows the need for a regular visitor no longer exists. In the small local prisons they are still welcomed and do good work.

nark. A policeman. Also one who gives information to the police; a 'copper's nark'. (From the Romany, 'nak'—nose.) See *bogey*.

needle, to. To express annoyance or irritation (service slang). Also, *browned off*, etc.

needles. Needles for making mailbags, etc., are issued to men in the shops and to those working in their cells. In many local prisons a careful check is kept on all needles, as on razor blades. Both are among the numerous articles men have been known to swallow in an attempt to commit suicide (see *suicide*). It is an offence to hold unauthorised needles in cell. See *mail-bags; palm*, etc.

New Hall Camp. Hutted camp attached to Wakefield Prison in Yorkshire. It accommodates about one hundred men. See *Wakefield; Prisons*.

Newchurch. Open-camp prison opened in 1949 on the Romney Marshes. Originally started with men from Aldington and Maidstone, it received prisoners direct from the London prisons. Located in a hutted camp, once used as a hostel. Closed for the time being. See *Prisons*.

news sheet. Before prisoners were allowed to have newspapers to read, a prison news sheet was printed at Maidstone and distributed to every prison in the country. It contained the main items of news, culled from *The Times* by a leader and vetted by the Deputy Governor. Other items concerned prison sports, games, etc., and there were articles on various popular subjects. See below.

newspapers. In many of the smaller prisons newspapers were not allowed until quite recently. The news was read out on Sunday after chapel service by the Governor. In some prisons such as Wormwood Scrubs where the 'stage' system is in force, the news is still read on Sundays for the benefit of short-term men who do not stay in long enough to qualify for 'stage'. Newspapers are issued in the dining-halls to men 'on stage', but one paper for about twelve men, with but an hour or two to read, leaves many unsatisfied.

Convicts on stage may have their local newspaper sent from home, and in the training centres ample newspapers are available. Some of the sensational papers are banned, but they are easily obtainable 'at a price'. (See *periodicals; censor; library*.) Newspapers are seldom censored nowadays, though at one time all reference to crimes were obliterated. This raised the value of a complete copy of the paper on the Black Market.

nick, the. Prison. The most commonly used slang word for any prison. See also *chokey; clink; digger.*

nicker, a. One pound sterling. See *bar,* etc.

night cans. In the ordinary prisons each prisoner is issued with a chamber pot in his cell, but in the *camps* (*q.v.*) night buckets were provided in each hut. It has been found, however, that men can be trusted not to 'wander' and now, in most camps, these insanitary articles have been abolished and those who wish may go freely to the proper lavatories. See *sanitation,* etc.

night screw. The officer in charge of a hall during the night. These men are generally old or for some reason considered unsuitable for day duty. They come on duty at about 9.30 p.m. and depart before unlocking time. For this reason the average prisoner never sees them and any trafficking between a night officer and a prisoner is limited to those privileged to stay up late or to be unlocked early. The night officer wears felt slippers and pads silently round the landings from key to key with his time recorder (*q.v.*). He carries a cell key in a sealed packet and in the event of an emergency should call the Orderly Officer. Only in cases of the utmost urgency may he open the sealed key packet. See *screw; landing; lights out; lock up.*

night-shirt. Having worn one shirt for a week, the prisoner is expected to use it for another week as a night-shirt. A clean shirt is issued him on bath days. Pyjamas are worn only in hospital. See *pyjamas; shirts; hospital.*

nine moon. Nine months' imprisonment. See *time*.

'nit nit.' 'Shut up.' 'Stop talking.' 'Be careful, someone is listening.' See *eye eye*.

no jet. 'Won't listen.' (See *bubble*. 'To put the bubble in the tube' = to put in a 'squeal', to tell tales. If there is 'no jet', then it means that the person told will not listen or will not take any action.) See *grass*.

No. 9 pill. Familiar old remedy for constipation. See also *medicine; hospital; M.O.*

noise. In the old convict prisons men become ultra-sensitive to noises. The wearing of felt slippers while in cell is compulsory, and normally when all men are locked in a heavy silence fills the whole prison. For this reason the slightest movement is noticeable in the buildings, which are built mainly of stone, slate, and steel. In the more modern prisons, with the introduction of radios, games, music practice, and now 'Music While You Work', the noise, amplified by the acoustically unsuitable buildings, is in keeping with modern times. To the sensitive man this is wearing on the nerves, a fact recognised by the medical officers, but until new buildings can be provided little can be done about it. In one or two instances it has been possible to fit out a 'Quiet Room' for the benefit of those who appreciate silence or the moderate playing of good music. See *radio*.

North Sea Camp. Borstal Institution with dormitory accommodation for 120. See *Borstal Institutions; Prisons*.

Northallerton. Men's prison. 207 cells. See *Prisons*.

Norwich. Local prison with accommodation for 177. See *Prisons*.

nosey. The prison censor. See *censor*.

Nottingham. Borstal Institution with cell accommodation for 185. See *Borstal Institutions; Prisons*.

nut. Head. See *loaf; nutting*, etc.

nut, a. A lunatic. One not 'all there'. See *hoppite; certified*.

nut, to do his. To lose all self-control. To go crazy. To smash up a cell. To go suddenly 'berserk'. When a man does any of these things he is spoken of as having 'done his nut'. See *bash up*.

nuthouse. Lunatic asylum. See *Broadmoor*, etc.

nutting. To use the head in a fight by suddenly smashing the top of it into an opponent's face. See *heading; putting in the leather; chiv*.

O

observation. A prisoner under observation is kept in one of the special cells set apart for the purpose. Remands, particularly those on murder charges or any charge where there is any question as to mental equilibrium, are always put under observation. See below.

observation cell. Differs from the ordinary cell in that there is a barred grille in the upper half of the door. This is covered by a hinged flap. With the flap down it is a simple matter for a passing officer to keep an eye on the occupant. The floor of the observation cell is frequently covered with cork or cork linoleum. It is used for many psychological cases—would-be suicides, epileptics, and so on. See *Peek; peep*.

office, to give the. 'To give him the office' = to initiate him into the running of things. To show a newcomer around.

officer. Lowest rank of the uniformed branch of the Prison Service. Formerly known as a 'warder' and still referred to as such by newspaper reporters. See *prison officer*. Also, *screw; flue; twirl; Chief; P.O.; Engineer; porter*, etc.

Officers' Club. Most prisons have their Officers' Clubs. These arrange social evenings; cricket matches and outings in the summer; dances, whist drives, and concerts in the winter. The big convict prisons, where the officers have their own villages, often have comfortable club-houses with cricket pitch and bowling green. Privileged prisoners tend these and also clean up the club-house—a coveted job, where cigarette ends abound and there is occasionally a partly filled beer bottle to be 'whipped'. See *Officers' Mess*.

Officers' Mess. Most prisons have an Officers' Mess, where officers living a long way off can get a meal, if not a drink. Jobs in the mess are much sought after by prisoners, for obvious reasons. The Officers' Mess is sometimes referred to as the 'screws' canteen'. See *Officers' Club*.

officers' quarters. As with all services nowadays the shortage of living accommodation is a cause of considerable concern and affects recruiting. Normally the prisons had ample accommodation and owned numerous houses nearby. Houses for senior members of the staff are always at hand, though many of them, like country vicarages, belong to a bygone era. Convict prisons form small communities of their own, where officers and their families seldom mix with 'outsiders'. See *prison officer*.

old geezer. Any old man (or woman). See *geezer; Pop*.

old lag. A recidivist. A convict who has served several sentences of penal servitude. See *lag; lagging; time; recidivist; emancipist.*

on appeal. A prisoner awaiting the outcome of an appeal against his sentence or verdict is spoken of as being 'on appeal'. His period of waiting does not count in his sentence and if the appeal fails he has that much extra time to serve. While 'on appeal' he has no special privileges.

on the run. Dodging the authorities. Wanted. A deserter from one of the services. See *trot, on the; run.*

oncer (R). One pound sterling. See *nicker.* (Pron.: wun-cer.)

'one away.' The cry that goes round the prison when a prisoner has escaped. The cry also constitutes an esoteric joke, based on the cry of officer or leader collecting a man from a working party. When taking a man from a shop or party the officer calls out to the instructor in charge, 'One away', meaning, one off the roll. On returning the man he calls, 'One back, sir.' (All officers address each other as 'sir'.) When there is an escape, or rumours of one, the grinning prisoners pass the news on with this cry. See *one on; over the wall; have it away.*

one D. One penny. See *D; deener.*

'one on.' When adding a man to a working party the officer calls out to the person in charge, 'One on, sir.' See *'one away.'*

'one ordinary bath.' Called out by the officer in charge of reception when a new arrival is ready for bathing. This indicates to the bath orderly that the man does not require a 'special bath'. See *bathing; special bath,* etc.

open-camp prisons. The prison of the future. A system of confining men within prescribed limits with a minimum of supervision, relying on trust. See *farm parties; Aldington; Wakefield*, etc.

open up. To unlock the cells. The morning opening-up starts at about 6.30 a.m., although cleaners, kitchen hands, etc., are released earlier. Officers or hall leaders go round the landings at 6 a.m. turning on the lights and calling out. The hall bell is rung and officers take up their positions. From his cell the prisoner can hear the voice of the Principal Officer or Orderly Officer calling out the landing numbers—thus: 'A.1'. The officer on A.1 landing has already counted the occupants on his landing. He calls that number back. 'A.2' and 'A.3' are called and so on, until all landing totals have been checked. If the number is correct, as it usually is, the Principal Officer then orders, 'Open up' or 'Unlock'. Comparative silence is then shattered by the rattle of keys, clanging of doors and iron-shod heels racing along stone and slate galleries. The first men unlocked reach the recess to empty their chamber pots. Other men fall in line. This is a moment to turn the average stomach and smoking is strictly prohibited. See *slop out; night screw; banged in; cell*, etc.

open visit. As distinct from a 'closed visit'. A prisoner may sit beside his visitors and is allowed to shake hands with them, kiss his wife or children, fondle the baby, etc. See *visits; closed visit; box visit; Zoo trip; drybath*.

Orderly Officer. Certain qualified officers perform this duty each 24 hours.

ordinaries. Ordinary prisoners. Men who are not convicts. See *stage; Special; leader*.

ordinary diet. The standard prison diet, as distinct from a special diet ordered on medical or religious grounds. See *diet; menu; religion*.

outfit. The paraphernalia used for an escape. 'He's got his outfit' = he has all the necessary impedimenta for an attempt to get over the wall and is awaiting a favourable opportunity. Would-be escapers, however, do not get far if they talk enough to have this said about them. See *escapee; over the wall; have it away.*

outside parties. Various parties work outside the walls. Gardeners tend flowers and vegetables at the houses of the Governor, Deputy, Chaplain, Chief Officer, etc. They also look after the Officers' Club and lawns. Building and Works parties tend the prison wall, pointing where necessary, and the painters visit those houses belonging to the prison and occupied by officers. This latter job is usually a good one, for cups of tea and even a slice of cake are often forthcoming. Wood-cutting and distributing parties also go out with their officers.

over the wall. An escape. In the event of a rumoured or actual escape, one man may ask another what has happened. The reply might be, 'So-and-so's gone over the wall' or 'He's had it away over the wall'. See *have it away; escapee.*

overalls. Overalls of different quality are issued for various tasks. Works party men and painters, etc., wear strong overalls which they can change at the P.W.S. when necessary. Tailors' shop men, carpenters, etc., wear a garment of thinner material. See *bluette; smock.*

overtime. Overtime is sometimes worked in the prison shops when there is a contract to be finished in a hurry. Men working overtime usually get a penny or two extra at the end of the week and are frequently given a few cigarettes by the instructor or officer in charge. They usually get a semi-unofficial issue of tea or cocoa. See *pay; labour; mailbags*, etc.

Oxford. Local prison for men, with cell accommodation for 118. See *Prisons.*

148

P

paddy. The padded cell. Used for violent cases. Often men who 'smash up', and who do not calm down immediately after, are given a spell in the paddy—or 'pads'—until they have cooled off. See *box; strong cell.*

Padre's Hour. Held once a week by the chaplain, along lines familiar in the services.

pads, the. Another name for the padded cell or *paddy* (*q.v.*).

pail, food. Also called diet tins; these are used for issuing food to men who eat in their cells or who are on special diets. There is a shallow dish which fits into the top and which is used for solids, while soup is contained in the actual pail. The newer pails are made of aluminium and so do not rust. Kitchen cleaning arrangements never being of a high standard, it is no uncommon thing in some prisons, to find the bottom of the old-type pail red with rust. The prison visitors, magistrates, etc., see only the specially polished pails kept on the shelves in the kitchen. The majority of Governors, Medical Officer's and Housemasters, however, give immediate attention to any complaints regarding cleanliness of food or food receptacles. See *diet.*

paint party. Party of prisoners who paint prison buildings, cells, etc. During the summer they are frequently engaged in repainting the officers' quarters, for which they use the standard prison colours—yellow, green, and brown. See *labour.*

painters. A whole-time class in painting and decorating is held in some prisons. Men learning this trade are helped to obtain similar employment on discharge. The use of browns, mottling, and imitation graining should give such men good qualifications for working on buildings belonging to public institutions. See *vocational training; education.*

palm. The ordinary leatherworker's or sailmaker's palm for sewing. Issued for sewing mailbags and similar articles. See *mailbags; cell task,* etc.

Palmolive. See *bath leader.*

pansy. A homosexual. An effeminate type. See *pouff,* etc.

paper. Cigarette paper. 'Give me a paper' = give me a cigarette paper. A packet of these costs one 'roll-up'. They may be sent in by friends, but those men who do not have them sent in buy them from those who do. In some prisons men are allowed to buy a packet on tobacco day. See *Rizla; A.G.; snout,* etc.

Parcel Post. Parcel Post mailbags are made in prison. They involve more work than the smaller type of mailbag, and for this reason are looked on with disfavour by some prisoners. See *mailbags.*

Parkhurst. Convict prison on the Isle of Wight. There is cell accommodation for 636 and a part is reserved for men undergoing preventive detention. There is also a large hospital with X-ray theatre. The officers have their own village nearby, and not far from the ex-'star' convict prison Camp Hill (*q.v.*). In days gone by Parkhurst was a centre for women and boys awaiting deportation to Botany Bay, etc., and the archives (see *muniment room*) show records of many cases of deportation for what are to-day considered trivial offences. See *Prisons; recidivist; P.D.*

pastimes. In many prisons, particularly the local or county, men spend long hours locked in their cells with very little or nothing to do. Reading palls and cell lighting is not too good. Many men cannot read; cell games may be prohibited or not available and study does not appeal to all.

The imaginative prisoner resorts to a number of pastimes. Cobbler's wax, used for waxing thread, provides scope for amusement. Many hours can be spent modelling. Men make little figures: a horse, a dog, a train, or a naked woman, or little gnomes and grotesque figures. Sometimes the models show humour, sometimes sadism, and, not infrequently, just plain lust. The psychologist could, no doubt, deduce a great deal from the distorted figures of men and women with organs fantastically warped and out of all proportion.

With wax a man can make many other things. Dice to roll along the floor; scraps of wood or chalk marking the pips. A dart can be made with wax and needle. Paper gliders, a sheet from the cell Bible or a library book and a knob of wax for the tip, will sail round the cell or out of the window opening.

When two friends occupy adjoining cells they sometimes play games with each other by tapping on the wall. The childhood game of 'battleships' can be played thus; the squares marked out on odd pieces of paper during the daytime. Draughts and chess can be played by a prearranged system of taps. There is no standard code for tapping; it is sometimes arranged privately on exercise ground or in the workshop. (See *quadratic alphabet; tapped signals.*)

The illiterate, denied the pleasures of reading, finds looking at pictures (geographic magazines usually) palls. He plays with what little there is in his cell. A few books, mug, plate, spoon, and so on, piled one on top of the other, become, to the imaginative, minarets and skyscrapers. Nail and hairbrush, soap dish and fork, strung together with sacking thread, become an express train roaring through the night— childish, of course, but it kills time.

In the up-to-date prisons and training centres there

is little or no need for such pastimes. A minimum of
time is spent in cell and there is plenty to occupy the
active mind. Even there, though, perhaps a man will,
on a sunny day, clamber on to his chair with mirror in
hand. If there is a block opposite and anyone looking
out of the window, an amusing half-hour can be spent
annoying him or provoking a return dazzle—an amusing
pastime, but one not to be tried on an officer. See
amusements; education.

Paterson, Sir Alexander, M.C., M.A. Late Prison
Commissioner who devoted most of his energies towards
prison reform. He is credited with improvements in the
management of Borstals and prisons alike. He wrote
numerous reports on Belgian, Dutch, and German
prisons and on 'Devil's Island'. He toured the peni-
tentiaries of the U.S.A., where he first got the idea of
the prison camp (*q.v.*), and later experimented with this
field by establishing the first British prison camp at
Wakefield (see *open-camp prisons*). He died at his home
in Chelsea in November 1947.

Paterson's Farm. See *Aldington; Prisons; open camps.*

patteran. The gipsy sign language.

pay. Partly due to the efforts of the Howard League
for Penal Reform, pay for convicts was introduced in
the '20's and later spread to ordinary prisons in 1934.
In those days one shilling would buy an ounce of
tobacco and one or two packets of cigarette papers.
To-day an ounce of cheap shag costs 3s. 4d. and
although the prisoner's pay has been increased by
50 per cent. it is still inadequate.

A prisoner usually starts off at 3d. a week, with which
he can buy 'roll-ups' (*q.v.*) or sweets. The maximum
pay is 1s. 6d. and is seldom given to men not engaged
on piece-work. There is a weekly deduction of ½d. or
1d. for the Common Fund (*q.v.*). A fixed sum is allotted

to each prison and as it is awarded by the Production Manager (*q.v.*) he is, naturally, loath to part with any that does not induce maximum production. In certain cases the Governor has arranged for top rate to be paid to non-productive workers, such as the senior Education Office leader, pay clerk and one or two shop leaders in responsible positions. See *snout; lob; stage; rhino*.

pay clerk. Redband or leader who assists the Production Manager with a certain amount of clerical work. His main duty is to keep the pay accounts and to assist the paying-out officer on pay and tobacco days. See *tobacco book; pay; snout*, etc.

pay, stage. In addition to the weekly pay, convicts are entitled to stage pay, for which they qualify after 18 months, on reaching the First Stage. After that they receive a weekly twopence extra for each year of sentence completed. A convict taken 'off' stage for punishment does not draw his pay until he is reinstated. See *convict; lagging*.

P.C. Previous conviction. A man with previous convictions is spoken of as having so many 'p.c.'s' to his credit.

P.C. Prison Commissioner. The Prison Commission. A Prison Commissioner pays periodical visits to each prison and a few days before his arrival there is great activity. Extra cleaning parties are put on to run wet rags over the landings and paintwork is dusted down. Prisoners have said that they can tell when the Commissioner is due by the food alone, even if there were no other signs. Prisoners may apply to see the Commissioner, but only on matters which cannot be dealt with by the Governor. See *V.C.*

P.D. Preventive detention. A sentence looked forward to by many old lags nearing the end of a term of penal servitude. P.D. can only be awarded to a man with a certain category of previous convictions and the exist-ing system has been amended by the passing of the Criminal Justice Act, 1948 (*q.v.*).

P.D. men wear a distinctive uniform: brown coat and corduroy trousers with a coloured tape down the seams. They are housed in Holloway (women) and Parkhurst (men). At one time there was accommodation for them at Camp Hill. Here they lived in 'flats'—two small blocks of tiny cells facing a courtyard which could be locked at night. They were given small allotments and what they cultivated they could sell to officers and others. They received about 5s. a week and were allowed numerous privileges denied convicts and prisoners. P.D. represented, for many, a form of security and such men needed little vigilance. They wanted to be 'in' and were frequently better off than inmates of workhouses whose only crimes were old age and poverty. See *recidivists*.

P.D. No. 1 and P.D. No. 2. Punishment Diet No. 1, bread and water, and No. 2, skilly at midday in addition to bread and water. Maximum consecutive P.D. is 3 days. On the fourth day a man sentenced to more than 3 days is given the ordinary diet before doing another three days on No. 1. Standard prison punish-ment for various infringements of rules has for many years been loss of remission (from a few days for minor offences to several months for such things as razor slashing), plus so many days on No. 1 and a week or more on No. 2 to follow. It is probable that this dietary punishment will be abolished. Most punishment is awarded for infringing rules regarding tobacco, the constant struggle between the staff and inmates. See *remission; punishment; snout.*

Peek, the, or **the peep.** The observation cell (*q.v.*). 'He's in the peek' = he is under observation. See *observation; Judas.*

154

peephole. The Judas. The small round hole or narrow slot in the cell door. It is covered with a strip of protective glass and a hinged metal flap, like that found over a keyhole, is fixed to the outside of the door. The glass is a safeguard for officers inspecting cells. Men have been known to run a pen or sharp stick into the eye of an officer when he looks in at checking-up time. It also prevents a man's friends passing in cigarettes while he is on punishment. The metal cover also has a minute hole punched in the centre and it is just possible for a man on the inside to squint through this at the corridor outside. When the glass is broken the flap can be worked back with stick or pen and messages whispered through to cleaners and others who have free movement about the landings. See *Judas*.

penal servitude. Penal servitude, dating from the days when prisoners could be deported to the Colonies has become obsolete with the passing of the Criminal Justice Act of 1948 (*q.v.*). For many years a sentence of penal servitude, or P.S., has meant nothing more than a slight difference in privilege allowed a long-term man and denied a prisoner. See *divisions; Criminal Justice Act*, 1948.

penman. A forger. Also *kite man*.

pens and ink. Pens and ink are kept by hall leaders and are issued, in the evening, on request. They must be returned before breakfast next morning. Writing facilities are usually available where men dine in association. Fountain pens are strictly prohibited. Ink, officially, may not be sent in for fear that the bottle might contain poison, drugs, or alcohol. Penholders and nibs are permitted. Prison penholders are usually very short, owing to the practice of cutting off lengths for making flint-holders. See *letters; correspondence courses; education; flints*.

Pentonville. London prison reopened for use by short-term offenders. See *Prisons.*

pepper. For fear that pepper might be thrown into a warder's face this commodity is used only in the kitchen. It can be bought from prisoners working in the kitchen and in a few instances is actually issued to tables for men on 'special stage'.

perform. To do a burglary. 'They picked me up before I had time to perform' = I was caught before I had time to start. See *screwing; drumming; villainy.*

periodicals. Weekly magazines and periodicals may be sent in by a man's friends or relations. Conditions and rules vary from prison to prison, but recently a Home Office order to all prisons was that such articles could be received only if sent from recognised newsagents and *not* by an individual. The reason for this is probably because pound notes had been found in some periodicals. In theory all magazines, papers, and books are examined by the library officer. Usually he has a leader or redband sitting next to him to record all literature received. One method of smuggling is to have a pound note folded into a popular periodical which is addressed to some unpopular prisoner. The library leader then acquires this magazine before the officer sees it. Should he fail to do so then the unpopular prisoner is due for a great deal of questioning. The lending of magazines, unless conducted through the library, is prohibited and old magazines are destroyed if found in a man's cell. This seems unnecessary, for no matter how old a book or magazine may be there is always someone who can derive pleasure from it. See *library; newspapers.*

Peter. A safe. 'To blow a Peter' = to open a safe with explosives. Also, anything that can be locked. Even a suitcase can be referred to as a Peter.

Peter. The most popular word (with 'flowery') for the prison cell (rhyming slang). See *flowery*.

Peterman. A safe-blower, cracksman, safe specialist. See *Peter; jelly; case; cane; perform*, etc.

petition. Every prisoner has the right to petition the Home Secretary. Nearly all prisoners send in at least one petition within a few months, or even weeks, of arrival in prison. There is, however, no chance at all of any reduction of sentence unless some new evidence comes to light or in the event of accident or illness, due to prison conditions. Apart from asking for remission, the chief object of petitions written by the ever-optimistic prisoner, a man may seek redress on some wrong, real or imaginary, ask to be allowed to conduct some business, to write a cheque, etc.

To many the actual petition form is a little puzzling. The front page contains instructions and the next three pages are lined with wide margins for Home Office notes. Capital letters warn the writer, 'Do Not Write Between the Lines'. This caution, however, is for those men who write, not evenly on the lines, but halfway between them.

To obtain a petition, application must be made to the Governor. The actual form, with a card of instructions and warnings of dire punishment in the event of frivolity or the use of obscene language, is given to the man in the evening. He must return it completed to an officer holding the rank of Principal Officer or higher. The petitioner then waits anything from a week or so to two or three months. He is then called up by the Governor and the reply is read out to him. The reply, particularly to those poignant pleadings for remission, usually starts, 'His Majesty's Secretary of State regrets . . .'

Bitter disappointment is usually felt at this reply, but optimism soon returns and within a few weeks the same man is up before the Governor, asking for another petition form. This time, he thinks, he will be lucky. See *bleat; scream; appeal.*

pewter. Silver. See *snow; white; pony in white.*

phoney. Not genuine, forged, counterfeit. This popular word, contrary to general opinion, is not imported from the U.S.A. It has been in use in our British underworld for over 200 years. The early form was *Phoney man* (or *phoneyman*)—a pedlar of imitation jewellery. Originally the word was *Fawney*, which referred to a real or imitation gold finger ring, the word coming from the Irish *fainné*, a finger ring. A *Fawney cove* was a man who practised the *Fawney rig*, the old dodge of 'ring dropping'.

phoney white. Counterfeit silver coins. Counterfeit banknotes. See *snide.*

photoframes. A man is allowed to have authorised photographs in frames, but he may not, officially, make them or have them made in prison. However, there is always a brisk trade in frames, which may be made of leather, in the bootshop or tailors', of wood in the carpenters', or of tin from the tinshop. The bookbinding shop or class also produces good frames. These are purchased for the usual 'roll-ups', and if the purchaser is lucky, remain in his cell. Periodically there are cell raids and all frames are confiscated. Sometimes men are punished, at other times they are merely admonished. In spite of this it is not long before the photographs are once again in frames of some sort. See *photographs.*

photographs. Prison rules allow a man to have up to four photographs in his cell. Any more in his possession must be placed in his 'property' (*q.v.*). The photographs must be of his friends or family and he is not allowed one of himself. Cuttings from magazines are prohibited, but this rule is, in the easier prisons, relaxed.

photographs for records. Are taken when a man is arrested or convicted and a few weeks before discharge. See *C.R.O.; discharge.*

pillows. A product of the canvas shop. See *mailbags; bagshop; mattresses; coir; flock*, etc.

pimp. One who touts for a prostitute on a commission basis. His association with women is purely commercial and in this respect he differs from a ponce. A pimp would be highly flattered were he called a ponce. See *ponce; Johnson*, etc.

pinhead. Popular nickname for anyone who has a particularly small head; particularly for a tall man with a seemingly small head.

pint pot. The regulation earthenware mug. See *P.P.*

plate-cloth. Wiping-up or drying cloth, given to men who eat in cell for use after washing their utensils. As a rule washing-up is limited to rinsing the porridge off the plate while 'slopping out' at the sink. The cocoa mug and fork and spoon can be washed with tea. The night's cocoa dissolves from the edges of the mug when hot tea is poured in and spoon and fork can be left to soak in the tea before it is drunk. The more fastidious afterwards rinse the articles in the washing-water jug and then dry them on the plate-cloth. See *cleaning materials; cell.*

P.O. Principal Officer. A senior rank, between that of Officer and Chief Officer, in the Prison Service. The P.O. assists the Chief Officer in the administration of discipline, etc. The Senior P.O. acts as Chief Officer during that official's absence. See *prison officer; screwdriver.*

P.O.A. Prison Officers' Association. The 'Warders' Trade Union'. An organisation which looks after the interests of prison officers; each prison has a representative and the organisation is now fairly strong. See *prison officer*.

points up—points down (R). Used by some prisoners to indicate whether tobacco is plentiful or scarce. Points up means that it is scarce and consequently worth more. Points down, there is plenty about and prices are low. See *snout; Findlay; baron*, etc.

pol. One who talks a great deal. (Short for 'Polly' or Parrot.) See *rabbits; bunny*.

polish, boot. A tin of boot polish and two or three old hairbrushes are placed on the exercise ground on Sunday at morning exercise. The first men to reach them are thus able to polish their shoes. Some prisons provide only dubbin. As usual with prison commodities, boot polish is always available for those who can pay. A tin of black polish is worth from two 'roll-ups' to about six. Since the war, with purchases of surplus Government clothing, etc., some shoes are brown. These have been roughly blacked over and many prisoners spend a great deal of time getting them back to their original colour. Brown polish costs considerably more than black, as it is not used in the prison and has to be smuggled in. See *P.W.S.; boots; shoes*.

polish, floor. Cell flooring is of wood, slate, or tiles. Floors must be scrubbed frequently and with wooden floors there is no alternative. Stone, slate, or tile floors may, unofficially, be polished and many men, particularly convicts, take great pride in keeping a high shine on their cell floors. Polish can be 'fiddled' through the stores and other sources or, most frequently, it can be made. Wax from the cobblers', or real beeswax from the tailors' shop, ochre from the painters'—who are also good for the turpentine—and a few minutes with a gas ring and a tin of polish is ready for the customer. See *cell*, etc.

polish, furniture. Cell furniture is made to be scrubbed and officially it may not be stained or painted. As with polished floors, numerous prisons turn a blind eye on the practice of staining tables, washstands, chairs, and so on, and in order to keep the articles smart the same sources are approached for furniture polish as for floor or shoe polish. It is easier to get Ronuk or some similar polish, as this is an issue. Hall or centre leaders use a certain amount and the chapel redbands usually have plenty—at a price. See *furniture; cell*, etc.

polish, to. 'To polish the apple' = to curry favour with the authorities by sycophancy. To put on a show of being busy. (From the costermonger's habit of rubbing the best apple on his sleeve but selling inferior ones.) See *grass; tube; bubble*, etc.

political offences. Political prisoners are never found in our prisons and there is no prison in the country reserved for them. The need is not there. During the late war the nearest approach to a political prison was the establishment of internment camps and reserved wings for 18*b* offenders. A great number of men, particularly in convict prisons, claimed that they were political prisoners and, by constantly talking about it, were able to influence many other prisoners into adopting an attitude of deference. These offenders were, for the most part, traitors; men who had broadcast for the enemy or who had flown our aircraft to enemy airfields with the deliberate intention of helping Germany. These men were nearly all members of Fascist bodies. Quite a number were ex-internees, no longer dangerous and for the most part obsessionists and men with petty grievances. One had made a hobby of burning haystacks in the belief that he was helping German bombers to hit our cities and factories. Another talked to all and sundry of the need for armed revolution. To a certain extent all were, in various degrees, dangerous at the time. The sentences awarded made quite sure they would do no harm, and yet considerable clemency was shown in numerous cases. One man, who offered help to the Germans through the Eire Ambassador, was released after a few months. Within weeks he repeated his offence. For the most part they fall into two definite categories: the weak, unpleasant type with a bee in his bonnet, and the intelligent supporter of his country's enemies who, had he done the same thing for the enemy, would have been shot out of hand. Those convicted by the civil courts mostly serve out their full sentences. Those imprisoned by courts martial frequently have their sentences considerably reduced. See *court martial*.

ponce. One who lives exclusively on the immoral earnings of women. He is able to exert some sort of 'charm' over them and would be deeply hurt were he to be called a pimp. See *Johnson; pimp; vice*.

ponce, to. To beg; to con; to scrounge. 'I ponced a smoke off the screw' = I begged a smoke from the officer.

pony. Twenty-five pounds. See *monkey; flim; ton*, etc., see below.

pony in white. Twenty-five shillings (in silver). See *white; pewter*, etc.

Pop. Any old man or man in the late forties (see *geezer; old geezer*). It is most common to address middle-aged and old men as 'Pop'. The younger the user of the word, the younger the man called 'Pop'. For a man in the late thirties to be called 'Pop' is a sign that the years are leaving their mark on him.

porridge. Summer and winter the regulation pint of porridge is issued at breakfast. See *diet*.

porter. A low rank in the Prison Service. Porters wear uniform but have not the same powers or privileges as the prison officer (*q.v.*). The stores are usually in charge of a porter.

Portland. Borstal Institution with cell accommodation for 359. This grim establishment is virtually cut off from the mainland and is an ideal place for training young men. See *Borstal Institutions; Prisons*.

pouff. The most commonly used word for a homosexual. See also, *iron hoof; brown hatter; 'she'*, etc.

power of attorney. No man sentenced to prison is allowed to carry on any form of business or to sign cheques, documents, etc. He may, however, petition the Home Secretary for permission to appoint a power of attorney. He is allowed special visits (*q.v.*) to discuss business matters with his lawyers, etc.

P.P. Pint pot. The standard earthenware mug.

Prescoed Camp. Attached to Usk Borstal Institution (*q.v.*).

printer, a. A typewriter.

printers' shop. The printing for the Prison Service is done mostly at Maidstone, where there is a big printing and bookbinding shop. Here it is possible to learn something about printing, stereo-blockmaking, and bookbinding. The latter is mostly limited to hand-bound account and form books, which by private enterprise would be machine-bound. See *Maidstone; bookbinding*.

prison officer. Every endeavour is being made to attract a different type of man to the Prison Service. The days of the bullying, loud-mouthed warder are numbered. The vast expense involved in the war against crime warrants every effort being made to use prison, as a punishment, as a last resort and where it must be awarded, to try to make useful citizens of its inhabitants.

Members of the regular Prison Service, mostly old-time warders with years of the service behind them, are somewhat opposed to the newcomers. Also there are still a number of 'War Reserve' officers and many 'probationers', and the 'officer class' of non-uniformed official is eyed with suspicion and distrust (see *Housemaster; Assistant Governor*). A prison officer starts with a probationary period, during which time he goes on to the Staff College at Wakefield. If he passes the tests there he is accepted into the Prison Service proper and, for the first few years, is liable to be 'bossed around' by his fellow-officers. All officers address each other as 'Sir' and there is a large gap between the ordinary prison officer and the next rank, that of Principal Officer. Service counts for a great deal and prestige depends entirely on it. After a number of years a smart man may be qualified as Orderly Officer (*q.v.*) or he can, by passing trade tests, become a tradesman officer as distinct from a disciplinary officer. He then qualifies for increased pay, which starts somewhere in the neighbourhood of £400 p.a., including allowances and extras. He may also be called on to do overtime, for which he is paid.

Those who reach the rank of Principal Officer have usually served from ten to fifteen years. Promotion after that is an even bigger step than from officer to P.O.—that is, to Chief Officer. Assistant Chief Officer or Deputy Chief is usually held by a P.O. Few Chief Officers are promoted to the non-uniformed branch and the Prison Officers' Association (P.O.A., *q.v.*) are doing their best to remedy this. Numbers of Chief Officers, however, have reached the rank of Deputy Governor or Governor, and in rare instances it has been known for a prison officer to reach the rank of Governor at an early age. Although very many prison officers are kind, understanding men with a genuine interest in the prisoners the present system of recruiting an Army officer class of young man into the non-uniformed branch is undoubtedly the best. It is too much to expect an old-time warder, with twenty or thirty years of shouting orders and locking and unlocking doors, to appreciate to the full an entirely new attitude towards offenders. A new and expensive system should not be jeopardised by allowing it to be run by men whose best years were spent in the old system which, by statistics alone, has proved such a dismal failure.

Other ranks in the uniformed branch include Hospital Officer, Engineer Officer, Officer Cook, etc. These rank mostly with the P.O. of the disciplinary side. See *screw*, etc.

prison rot. General deterioration, particularly mental, which frequently sets in after a varying period of imprisonment. Some men are affected by prison rot after a very few years; others serve anything up to about fifteen years with never a sign of it. Strain and worry are the chief causes. Prison rot affects different men in different ways; as a rule they become surly and depressed, avoid their fellows, and often talk to themselves. See *cobitis; convictitis; debtor's colic; gate fever; whanker's doom.*

Prisoners' Aid Societies. See *D.P.A.; N.A.D.P.A.S.; Central Association.*

Prisoners' Family Aid. See above, also *Church Army*.

Prisons and Borstal Institutions. The following is a list of establishments given in the Report of the Commissioners for 1948.* It must be borne in mind that

* Acknowledgment is made to H.M. Stationery Office for permission to quote from the Commissioners' Report.

new prisons, camps, and training centres, etc., are still being opened.

Local Prisons:

	Cells		Other Accommodation		Total	
	Men	Women	Men	Women	Men	Women
Aldington	—	—	60–100		60–100	
Askham Grange	—	—	—	60	—	60
Bedford	120	—	24	—	144	—
Birmingham (Winston Green)	375	87	24	—	399	87
Bristol	209	—	16	—	225	—
Brixton	591	—	—	—	591	—
Canterbury	167	—	—	—	167	—
Cardiff	218	65	—	—	218	65
Chelmsford	95	—	60	—	155	—
Dartmoor	See under Convict Prisons.					
Dorchester	133	—	—	—	133	—
Durham	474	105	—	—	474	105
Exeter	197	37	4	3	201	40
Gloucester	117	—	100	—	217	—
Holloway	—	644	—	63	—	707
Leeds (Armley)	477	—	—	—	477	—
Leicester	203	—	—	—	203	—
Lewes	289	—	—	—	289	—
Lincoln	293	—	100	—	393	—
Liverpool (Strangeways)	705	—	—	—	705	—
Maidstone	350	—	65	—	415	—
Manchester	707	269	—	—	707	269
Northallerton	151	—	56	—	207	—
Norwich	137	—	40	—	177	—
Oxford	118	—	—	—	118	—
Pentonville	640	—	—	—	640	—
Reading	172	—	—	—	172	—
Shrewsbury	165	—	—	—	165	—
Stafford	645	—	36	—	681	—
Swansea	161	—	—	—	161	—
Wakefield	782	—	100	—	882	—
Wandsworth	922	—	—	—	922	—
Winchester	279	—	116	—	395	—
Wormwood Scrubs	1,139	—	—	—	1,139	—

Convict Prisons:

	Cells		Other Accommodation		Total	
Dartmoor	800	—	—	—	800	—
Holloway	See under Local Prisons.					
Aylesbury	See under Borstal Institutions.					
Ley Hill	—	—	288	—	288	—
Parkhurst	636	—	—	—	636	—

166

Preventive Detention Prisons:

Holloway	See under Local Prisons.
Parkhurst	See under Convict Prisons.

Borstal Institutions:

	Cells		Other Accommodation		Total	
	Men	Women	Men	Women	Men	Women
Aylesbury	—	218	—	—	—	218
Borstal	254	—	75	—	329	—
Camp Hill	351	—	—	—	351	—
Chelmsford	157	—	—	—	157	—
Dartmoor			See under Convict Prisons.			
Durham			See under Local Prisons.			
East Sutton Park	—	—	—	37	—	37
Exeter			See under Local Prisons.			
Feltham	150	—	272	—	422	—
Gaynes Hall	—	—	122	—	122	—
Hewell Grange	—	—	139	—	139	—
Hollesley Bay Colony	—	—	332	—	332	—
Holloway			See under Local Prisons.			
Huntercombe Place	142	—	—	—	142	—
Latchmere House	141	—	—	—	141	—
Lowdham Grange	—	—	204	—	204	—
North Sea Camp	—	—	120	—	120	—
Nottingham	185	—	72	—	257	—
Portland	359	—	—	—	359	—
Usk	113	—	100	—	213	—
Wandsworth	169	—	—	—	169	—
Totals	14,488	1,425	2,465	163	16,953	1,588

The above accommodation excludes all special accommodation, such as for V.D., itch, punishment, etc. In a number of prisons it has been necessary to put three men to one cell. Complete statistics can be found in the Official Report.

In addition to the foregoing the following have now been opened:

Preston Prison.

Portsmouth (Kingston), opened for Borstal inmates whose licences have been revoked.

Sudbury Park, Derbyshire. Hutted camp.

Chelmsford Prison. Part reserved for Borstal revokees now reverts to men's prison.

Prisons, Scottish. The Commissioners for Prisons and Directors of Convict Prisons are responsible only for those in England and Wales. Scottish prisons have their own administration according to Scottish laws and are not included here.

prisons without bars. See *open-camp prisons; farm parties; Wakefield; Aldington; Maidstone*, etc.

private study. In those prisons where educational classes are laid on, men are permitted to study in their cells and many prefer this to attending classes. Men on approved courses may have their cell lights on an hour later and may keep pens and ink in cell. See *correspondence courses; education; Maidstone*, etc.

probation. More and more use will be made of the existing probation system. Where first offenders and, in particular, young men and women are concerned prison will be awarded only if probation is considered unsuitable. A large number of new probation officers have been enrolled and parties of them are shown over the prisons where they can get some small insight into the present-day system. See *Criminal Justice Act*, 1948.

production. So far as the Production Manager (*q.v.*) is concerned, all prison shops work with an eye on production and attempt to beat their previous records. Handicapped by an antiquated system, much work that could be performed by machine is done by hand. Much more could be done by prison labour and prisons could be self-supporting. Articles turned out now include: mailbags, hammocks, ships' fenders and coaling sacks, bags for the Mint, suits for naval cadets, prison furniture, woven cloth for making into prison clothing, execution equipment boxes and a variety of other articles. See *labour*, etc.

Production Manager. The Production Manager is a civilian who works, more or less, on his own. He supervises the production of the prison shops, advises on matters connected with all production. All prison pay is arranged by him and he usually allots the prices for piece-work. He is assisted by a leader or redband pay clerk (*q.v.*) and is in constant touch with the Home Office. All contracts are passed to him and he is responsible for their proper fulfilment. See *prison officer*, etc.

property. A prisoner's possessions, such as his clothes, suitcase, pipe, and other small personal belongings (see *valuables*). These are kept at *reception* (*q.v.*) by the Reception Officer. Strictly speaking, a man entering prison is allowed nothing but the official clothes he stands up in. Anything permitted, such as pipe, cigarette papers, a photograph, a letter kept for sentimental or business reasons, must first be applied for (see *applications, Governor's*). Permission having been granted, the man is duly called up to reception, where the article is given him. He signs for it in one of the many books which form an integral part of the prison system. See *photographs*, etc.

P.S. Penal servitude. See *time; lagging; Criminal Justice Act,* 1948; *penal servitude.*

psychiatric unit. This unit operates at Wormwood Scrubs, where prisoner patients are received from prisons all over the country. Once the psychiatrist was unable to attend more than a few hours a week; now he is resident and the importance of this side of medicine is receiving more and more attention. In other prisons there are Medical Officers who have a genuine interest in the subject and, using what knowledge they have, do their utmost to help prisoners. However, it is a branch which, for various reasons, has been neglected. It is necessarily expensive and, as prison medical officers will confirm, made doubly difficult by the surroundings. It is hard to imagine much satisfactory progress being made in such soulless surroundings as

Wormwood Scrubs. That the whole subject is of increasing importance is shown by the Commissioners' Reports and consequently the future outlook is good. Furthermore, there is every indication that future offenders will have psychiatric attention *before* committal and that evidence by qualified psychiatrists will be accepted with less reserve. See *Criminal Justice Act,* 1948.

P.T. Young prisoners and convicts are given compulsory P.T. by qualified officers. In addition there are, in several prisons, voluntary classes in P.T. and gymnastics and these are always well attended. Frequently older men, exempt from the compulsion rule, join in the P.T., which is held on the exercise yard, in view of men on exercise. (See *gymnastics; Y.P., Y.C.*)

The Central Council of Physical Recreation, who have provided teachers for P.T. classes in women's prisons, have organised a course for P.T. instructors from the Prison Service.

punishments. Punishment for breaches of prison discipline has for long been confined to dietary punishment and loss of remission for lesser offences; and the birch or cat for those involving violence (see *P.D. No. 1 and No. 2; corporal punishment*). The whole question of punishment is under review and there is every indication that the existing system will be radically changed.

pussy. The cat-o'-nine-tails. See *cat; corporal punishment; get your back scratched; apron,* etc.

put the bubble in. To put in a 'squeal' or 'squeak'; to inform; to 'grass'. See *grass; bubble; no jet; tube,* etc.

putting in the leather. Kicking an opponent in a fight; particularly after he has been knocked down. See *heading; nutting.*

P.V. Prison visitor. See *N.A.P.V.*

P.W.S. Part Worn Stores. Known among many prisoners as the 'Well Worn Stores'. All clothing, footwear, bedding, soap, etc., is issued from the P.W.S. Dirty clothing is collected by them and handed over to the laundry (*q.v.*).

Men working in the P.W.S. are in an excellent position to 'sell' new clothing and can always be relied on for the best shoes, socks, underwear, etc., provided tobacco is forthcoming. See *bathing; cell; fumigator.*

pyjamas. Pyjamas are issued only in hospital. All men use an ordinary shirt after it has been worn during the daytime for one week. See *shirts; night-shirt.*

Q

quadratic alphabet. This alphabet seems to be an international one used by prisoners to communicate with each other by means of tapping on the walls or heating pipes. It is not, however, in use in England, though English prisoners have experimented with it. Such means of communication are unnecessary in the modern prison.

A message tapped on the water pipes can be heard in any cell on the same floor, and even in cells above or below. Occasionally men arrange signals among themselves; perhaps to indicate that a certain 'fiddle' went off all right. Such signalling is unpopular and if prolonged will cause great commotion from those men who want to read or sleep. Messages tapped on walls, where there is no pipe, can be transmitted round an entire prison so long as there is not an empty cell to break the sequence. The quadratic alphabet is easily memorised and a little practice allows considerable speed to be attained. For example, to transmit the word 'escape'—*one* tap indicates the *first line*; after a very slight pause *five quick taps* indicate the *fifth* letter on that line, 'E'. Next, four taps, slight pause, another four taps—fourth line, fourth letter, 'S'. And so on, with a longer pause between words. There is a definite urge to communicate with others among men locked in for long hours. (See *pastimes.*) Men frequently arrange to call 'Good night' to each other through

A	B	C	D	E
F	G	H	I	J
K	L	M	N	O
P	Q	R	S	T
U	V	W	X	YZ

the window vents, at a fixed hour, or to tap, whistle, or even drop something at a time when both can listen. Thus they feel that they are not alone, even though they be locked in. (See *swinging the line.*) In a very different category are the love letters passed between homosexuals, but the same basic idea is probably there. See *love letters.*

Quasimodo (R). The chapel redband. Prisoner who is responsible for cleaning the prison chapel. (From Lon Chaney's 'Quasimodo' in the film of *The Hunchback of Notre Dame.*) See *redband; Gabriel.*

queen (M). See *pouff.*

queenie (M). *Idem.*

queer, a. One with homo- or bi-sexual tendencies. This word is quite as popular as *pouff.* When speaking of the unnatural habits of another it is also usual to refer to him as being 'queer'.

queer quartet (R). See *death watch*.

quod (O). (Also, 'quad'.) Prison. From 'quadrangle'. See *clink; chokey; nick*, etc.

R

rabbit, to. To talk a great deal. One who 'rabbits' all the time is one who never stops talking. To have a 'rabbit' = to have a pow-wow. (Probable origin: the huddling together, like young rabbits.) See *bunny; pol*.

rabbits. In Merchant Navy slang refers to any small articles of contraband but not to smuggling proper. A Customs officer might ask a shore-going seaman, 'How many rabbits have you got?' He refers to little articles, usually taken ashore as presents and which it is hoped will not be taxed or confiscated.

radio. Nearly all the larger prisons have radio installed. In some prisons the programmes are centrally controlled and given over loud-speakers in the cell blocks for half an hour or so in the evening. The acoustic properties of the cell blocks do not lend themselves to this form of entertainment. Where men are in association, in halls or dining-rooms, there is a radio set which may be turned on at specified hours. The almost non-stop jangling of the radio, always on too loud and badly distorted, is a source of considerable discomfort to many. Few men are interested in anything but football, racing results, and jazz. The man who would like to listen in comfort to a programme is unlucky. Prison Medical Officers are aware of the abuses of radio and the distress the noise can cause, but there is little that can be done about it until there is enough accommodation to allow for separate listening rooms, etc. News bulletins, though always switched on, are rarely listened to, except for sports news and for, in 1948, news of the progress of the Criminal Justice Bill. In 1949 Maidstone introduced 'Music While You Work', relaying 'music' to the workshops over a loud-speaker system. Although this is in keeping with the present-day trend towards a world of noise, it must inevitably cause distress to many. See *amusements; concerts*, etc.

radio car. See *Sweeney; holler wagon*, etc.

radio hobbies. Some prisons are able to allow a limited number of men to learn to make and repair radio sets, and at Maidstone, where one or two skilled radio technicians were lodged, a course in Radio Maintenance Engineering was conducted with some success. The officer in charge of electrical installations also takes classes in Electricity and Radio. Radio sets are not allowed in cells except in rare circumstances and then only by authorisation of the Medical Officer.

raid. A special search of cells or workshops for prohibited articles. These raids usually follow when some 'racket' has been uncovered or when it is noticed that there is a great deal of tobacco about the prison. Officers are quick to note when men are smoking a great deal and frequently on canteen day ('snout day') as much as twice the amount of money is spent as that paid out. These 'raids', conducted by every available officer, are in addition to the usual routine cell searches. All searches are recorded in a special book printed for the purpose. As a rule there is warning of a raid, even though it be but a few minutes. This generally allows time for hidden contraband to be disposed of. See *search; Search Book; turnover; drybath.*

rat. A dwelling-place or lodging. See *drum; gaff; lumber*.

rattler, the. Any railroad train. A man due for release in a few days will talk incessantly of catching the 'very first rattler out of town'.

razor blades. Shaving facilities vary considerably from prison to prison. In the small prisons men are shaved in the workshops or they may be given razor and rusty blade by the barber. They shave from a bucket of warm water while he cuts hair. He then collects all blades, etc., for which he is responsible.

In the better or more modern prisons men may have razor blades sent in by their friends. To stop trafficking (a blade is worth a 'roll-up') no man is allowed more than one blade at a time. Each Saturday he may obtain a new one by surrendering the old one to the Principal Officer.

Occasionally, even in the best prisons, there is an outburst of razor-slashing. It is then necessary to penalise all men by the withdrawal of all blades and razors. These are then issued at certain hours. Shaving is usually carried out in cold water, though in some prisons the cleaners carry buckets of hot water round when officers are serving tea or the 8 p.m. cocoa. Men may then have a shaving mug of hot water. Where hot water is not available men frequently shave in tea, which is always hot if not too strong. See *hot water; shaving; ablutions; chiv*.

R.C. Roman Catholic. All prisons have facilities available for Roman Catholic worship. Priests are usually part-timers from nearby churches. The percentage of Roman Catholics in prison is high, though there is no apparent reason for this. See *religion; chapel*, etc.

reader. Book, magazine, or newspaper. 'Let's have a darry at your reader' = let me have a look at your book.

Reading. Local prison, recently reopened. Oscar Wilde wrote his famous Ballad here. Now used as a "classification" centre. See *Prisons; literary efforts.*

ready or **'eddy.** Ready cash, under £5 in value. One of those words which a certain type of man likes to clip. Such as 'fick 'un' for 'thick one'. See *crackle; white; fick 'un.*

rec. Used in some prisons instead of the word 'association'. The prisoners' recreation time. See *association.*

receiver. One who deals in stolen property. See *fence; swordsman; granny.*

reception. Prison department where new arrivals are fitted out, their private belongings stored (see *property*), and where discharges have their final prison bath, collect their clothes, and are given their personal possessions. Clothing for new arrivals is brought here by men from the P.W.S. (*q.v.*) and the uniforms of discharged men are taken by them to the laundry. In a prison where there is a remand block the jobs in reception are much sought after. Remands always have plenty of tobacco and trafficking is easy. A prisoner working in reception, usually a leader, is able to traffic in clothing, etc. See *inspection, Medical Officer's; P.W.S.; property; discharge; bath.*

reception, a. A new arrival.

reception kit. On reception into prison a man is issued with uniform, shoes, tie, and underwear. He is given two shirts, two sheets, towel, pillow-slip, toothpowder tin, soap, hair-brush, comb, nail-brush, cell slippers, and the first two books that come to hand. If he has any tobacco or cigarettes when he arrives he can be sure of getting good things; otherwise he takes what comes. Everything is crammed into the pillow-slip, which he carries with him from place to place until he is finally shown a cell. By this time the pillow-slip, having been left on various floors while he interviews Medical Officer, Hall Officer, Orderly Officer, and so on, is ready to be turned inside out for use. It will have to last him at least a week, more probably a fortnight. See *cell; bathing kit; P.W.S.*, etc.

reception letter. On arrival into prison a man is entitled to a reception letter to enable him to keep his family informed of his whereabouts. It is usually issued automatically without having to make special application. See *letters; visits; special letter; applications, Governor's.*

receptions. Men newly received into prison. The leader i/c reception may be asked, 'How many receptions to-night?' In small local prisons men are coming and going almost daily. In the convict prisons and training centres men are received about once a week or fortnight, usually on a Friday or Tuesday.

recess. The lavatory and urinal, which are generally situated in a recess (two cells knocked into one). There is usually one slop-sink—though this is absent in many prisons even to-day—and one w.c. per landing. This accommodates anything from twenty to thirty or more men. See *slop-out; yard lavatories*, etc. Lavatories are always referred to as 'the recess'.

recidivist. An habitual criminal. The new Criminal Justice Act of 1948 will drastically alter the treatment of these men. The old system of preventive detention will be considerably modified. See *P.D., Parkhurst; Camp Hill; old lag; lag; lagging; copped a packet; emancipist; Holloway.*

red. Gold. Gold ornaments, such as bracelets, rings, etc. See *white; pewter; reddite.*

red collar. The forerunner of the redband. In the 'old days' one or two trusted prisoners were allowed a certain amount of freedom of movement about the prison. So that they could easily be identified they wore red collars to their coats and red on sleeves and lapels. They were sometimes referred to as 'devils' (*q.v.*). To-day the redband is a common sight in most prisons.

red, in the. In the money. Money (red—gold) is coming in easily. (See above.)

redband. A privileged prisoner. He is allowed to travel freely about the prison in pursuance of his duties. For this purpose he is given a red armband to wear. He must hand this in at the end of his working day. Only leaders (*q.v.*) are allowed freedom of movement after labour hours. The redband is the outcome of the 'red collar' (*q.v.*) or 'trustie' (*q.v.*) of the old days. Cleaners, food orderlies, gardeners, yard cleaners, etc., are given redbands. See *stage; leader; red collar; trustie*, etc.

reddite. A jeweller. (One who handles gold.) See *red*.

Reform Bill. See *Criminal Justice Act*, 1948.

religion. Freedom of worship is allowed to all denominations. The official religion is Church of England, but R.C.'s, Nonconformists, Jews usually have their own places of worship in the prison. Eastern religions are allowed special food according to their beliefs and are not expected to attend chapel parade. See *chapel; Jew; R.C.*

remand, a. One held in custody awaiting trial. He is not a prisoner, in that he is 'innocent until proved guilty'. The few privileges allowed him make a thin line of distinction between remands and prisoners. If he has money he is allowed to buy 100 cigarettes a week or two ounces of tobacco. He may have meals sent in and is allowed a pint of beer with his dinner. Usually he is allowed to wear his own clothes; if not he is issued with a brown uniform. He may write as many letters as he likes and may have a visit every afternoon. He is housed in a special block to avoid contact with prisoners with whom he might traffic. If he has no money he is permitted to work (sew mailbags) and may earn up to 6*d.* a day and not more than 3*s.* a week. See *layabout; laydown; browncoat; deport*, etc.

remanet. A remainder. Part of an unexpired sentence. A convict who breaks parole when on licence is obliged to serve the remanet of his sentence. See *time; ticket; lagging.*

remission. With the outbreak of World War II, the amount of remission for convicts and prisoners was made the same, and increased to one-third of the sentence. It applies to any sentence of more than one month, except in the case of 'life' or 'H.M.P.' (*q.v.*). It is very unlikely that the old system will be reverted to. That was, for prisoners one sixth remission, and for convicts one-quarter. (See *stage; P.D. No.* 1 *and No.* 2.) Remission can be forfeited by bad conduct.

Report, Commissioners'. Periodically the Stationery Office publish the *Report of the Commissioners for Prisons and the Directors of Convict Prisons.* This can be obtained for a shilling or two and deals largely with statistics. Included are reports of new buildings, Governors' and Medical Officers' reports, and the general outline of progress for the period concerned.

report, on. On a charge. If a man is guilty of any breach of rules, etc., he is 'put on report' and, in due course, appears before the Governor. See *case, to.*

reprieve. See *executions; murderers; manslaughter; H.M.P.; lifer.*

179

restraints. Belt and cuffs are kept for emergencies. In the 'old days' a man likely to prove violent wore a long cape to hamper his movements. Violent types of men are now sent to a suitable prison. See *darbies; paddy*.

rhino. Pay, money, cash. It is possible that here there is a connection with the popular word 'snout', for tobacco. See *snout; pay; lob*.

R.I.C. Rest in cell. A card bearing this lettering is hung on the door if a man reports sick or is ordered to bed. Maximum period R.I.C. is three days. If not fit then a man is sent to hospital (*q.v.*).

Richard. A girl. The girl friend. (From rhyming slang, Richard the Third—bird.) See *bird; tart*, etc.

ring the changes. To cheat; to defraud. To 'pull a fast one'. To pass counterfeit money. To 'con'. See *con, to; knock*.

ringer, the. The prison hall bell. Any bell. See *bell*.

ringmaster (R). The officer in charge of the centre. See *centre; centre screw*.

Ritzie. Showy, flashy, classy. 'A Ritzy tart' = a smart, flashily dressed girl. See *Richard; Jane; bride*, etc.

Rizla. A popular brand of cigarette paper. 'Gimme a Rizla' = please let me have a cigarette paper. See *paper; A.G.; snout*.

In most prisons men are allowed to have a certain number of packets of cigarette papers sent in by friends. Cigarette papers are usually in great demand by the 'Findlays' or 'barons', who use a great number in the manufacture of 'roll-ups'. A packet of papers is worth one 'roll-up'. See *snout*.

rocks (R). Diamonds. More popularly referred to as 'ice' (*q.v.*).

rod. Common Americanism affected by youths of a certain type when speaking of a revolver or automatic pistol. See *heater; Roscoe*.

rofe. Four years' penal servitude. See *time; lagging*.

roll-up. Hand-made cigarette. A 'good' roll-up is one that has a reasonable amount of tobacco in it; a 'thin' roll-up is one containing the very minimum of tobacco (known respectively as a 'fick 'un' and a 'fin 'un'). An esoteric joke about the 'fin 'uns' is to ask the seller if he threaded a strand of tobacco through the paper with a needle. See *baron; Findlay; tailor-made; bacco; buy; sell; trafficking; snout*.

Roman candle. A Roman Catholic.

rootie. Service word for food or meals. See *grub*.

rope, the. Hangman's rope. In England a new rope is used for each execution. In the Colonies the same rope is used over and over again and is, when necessary, repaired. The making of hangmen's ropes is carried on by the firm of John Edgington, in the Old Kent Road. See *executions; hangman; top*, etc.

roping. The process of sewing a stiffening rope, usually coir, round the top of a mailbag. See *mailbags; cell tasks*, etc.

Rory or **Rory O'Moore.** Door. Cell door. (Rhyming slang.)

Roscoe. Automatic pistol. See *heater*.

round-up. A thorough search for prohibited articles (see *raid*, etc.). Also, a more or less routine search for articles of clothing. Frequently men who 'buy' clean shirts, handkerchiefs, pairs of socks, etc., throw the dirty ones into any odd corner. Officers engaged in rounding up these can rarely pin the blame on any one man. See *search*.

Rowton Houses. Cheap lodging-houses to be found in London and most big cities. See *doss-house; kip*, etc.

rub him out. To get rid of somebody. Not necessarily by foul means. One who is always telling tales and upsetting a quiet little 'racket' can be rubbed out by being given a thrashing or a beating up in the 'recess'. Also, 'I don't want to know him'—which is self-explanatory.

ruck. To make a row; to create a disturbance; to get into trouble.

rugmaking. Introduced into many prisons as a hobby and as occupational therapy. Although shortage of materials limits the number of men who can take up this pastime, it is extremely popular and in some cases men are allowed to do this work in their cells. Rugs are sold in aid of the hobbies fund in order to purchase more materials, wool, felt, etc. See *hobbies; Maidstone*.

rumours. All prisoners seemed blessed with a spirit of supreme optimism. Rumours, always rife in prison, spread with amazing rapidity and grow wilder and more lurid with each telling. All prisoners, though many would hotly deny it, are certain in their own minds that they will never have to serve the full sentence required by law. Any one of a dozen things, they are certain, will bring an immediate release. See *special release*.

The Reform Bill (see *Criminal Justice Act*, 1948) caused an endless succession of rumours. A few of the more popular ones, all of which were to bring release, were: that a parole system would be introduced; that remission would be increased from one-third to two-thirds; or that all remission would be increased to one-half. Immediately after the war 99 per cent. of prisoners were convinced that there would be an amnesty, unheard of in the British system. When the Royal Family toured South Africa the rumours said that there would be, if not an amnesty, then a substantial remission, (*a*) when they left, (*b*) when they returned. Similar rumours continued up to the time of the birth of the prince and will go on until the day when there are no prisons or prisoners. In many ways these rumours do a great deal of good. Like petitions to the Home Secretary, asking for remission in plaintive terms, the prisoner has something to look forward to. Disappointment does not last: there is always a new rumour to take its place. See *amnesty; remission; Criminal Justice Act,* 1948; *petition.*

run, on the. Deserting from the services. Avoiding the law. A man who has escaped from prison, or who is wanted by the police, is 'on the run'. See also *trot, on the; bat.*

R.W.V. Robbery with violence. See *G.B.H.*, etc.

S

safe screw. Prison officer who can be trusted to co-operate in illicit dealings. One who, if not willing to traffic, will not say anything to his superiors. One who turns his back on minor 'fiddling', etc. See *screw; bent screw; trafficking*, etc.

safe twirl. See above.

safety net. The steel nets spread across the hall, from landing to landing on the first floor, to prevent accidents, attempts at homicide, suicide, etc. See *hall; block; landing; suicide.*

salt. An earthenware salt cellar and lid is part of the standard cell equipment where men do not eat in dining-halls. Salt is taken from a large box placed on the centre. This is kept filled by the hall leader (*q.v.*) or centre leader (*q.v.*). See *pepper.*

salts. A man in need of a laxative need not report 'sick'. A box of Epsom salts is kept on a table in the centre and the man may help himself. Sometimes hot water may be obtained from the hall or centre leader, otherwise the salts may be taken in tea or cocoa. See *toothpowder*.

Salvation Army. Members of this body visit the prisons and do a great deal towards providing entertainment in the way of feature films (*q.v.*) and concerts. See *Booth; religion; Church Army*.

sanitation. In all prisons this is of the crudest, and in the halls lavatory accommodation is generally hopelessly inadequate. See *karzy; slop-out; recess*.

scabies. More prevalent in some prisons than in others and always looked out for by prison Medical Officers. Men with scabies are housed in special cells which are later fumigated. All bedding and clothing is fumigated, for which purpose it is removed by men from the P.W.S., one of whom is usually in charge of the fumigator. See *itch pitch; isolation cells; cimex lectularius; fumigator*.

scabies library. A small library is usually kept for men suffering with scabies. The books may not be handled by other prisoners. See also *T.B. library; V.D. library*.

scarper. To escape; to run away; to 'beat it'. See *have it away; over the wall*, etc.

schnide. Also spelt *snide* (*q.v.*). From the Yiddish, meaning 'phoney'.

schpieler. A gaming-house. See *gaff*.

score. Twenty pounds. See *pony; monkey; flim; ton*, etc.

scratched. Given the 'cat'. See *get your back scratched*.

scratcher. A match. 'Got a scratcher?' = have you a match?

scream. An appeal. 'He put in a scream' = he appealed against the finding of the court. Also, *squawk; bleat*.

184

screw. Prison officer. All prison officers (warders) are spoken of as 'screws', by both prisoners and the officers themselves. The word derives from the days when keys were carried on a huge ring, before the invention of the modern ward lock; the key operated with a screwing motion, similar to the existing keys for handcuffs. See also *flue; prison officer; twirl; P.O.; Chief*, etc.

screw, to. To burgle. 'He screwed a gaff last night' = last night he burgled a house. See *gaff; drum; screwsman*.

screw up. To lock up. 'I'll screw up before I leave' = I'll lock up before I go. See *chubbed in; milned in; banged up*, etc.

screwdriver. Principal Officer, but sometimes used when speaking of the Chief Officer or Governor. When either of these is a strict disciplinarian and always 'driving the screws'—or officers—he is called a screwdriver. See *screw*.

screwing. Burgling. 'He was done for screwing' = he was charged with burglaring.

screwsman. A burglar, housebreaker. One who specialises in burglaries only. See *Peterman; screw, to*, etc.

scrub it. Forget it. Let it go; don't say any more. I don't believe you.

scrub-out. To have a thorough clean-out of one's cell. To scrub the floor. A man whose cell is considered dirty by the inspection officer may be ordered to 'have a good scrub-out'.

Search Book. One of the many books kept in prisons. Every search, whether of a whole cell block or of an individual prisoner, must be entered in this book, together with details of anything found. See *below*.

search, routine. Cells are searched at more or less regular intervals and all confiscated articles registered in the Search Book (*q.v.*). Nearly all prisons have officers employed daily in going from cell to cell, but a favourite system is to order all men in a block to go to their cells and to lock themselves in. As many officers as can be spared then go to each cell in turn. The prisoner is stripped and his cell turned inside out. Officers in the grounds watch the windows for anything that may be thrown out. A certain amount of amusement can be derived by flicking scraps of rolled-up paper and other rubbish through the window opening. Watching officers are obliged to inspect these and as new officers always get this detail they are usually full of zeal. If, of course, a man can be identified as being responsible for this form of amusement, he is automatically punished.

Officers search in pairs and if anything is found the Principal Officer is called in. The man and his cell are then subjected to an even closer search. The object of all searching is to find money and letters (see *stiffs*) and tobacco. Although well organised these searches usually fail to catch the big barons (*q.v.*). Only a few minutes' warning is necessary and 'hot' goods can be jettisoned.

Searches on a big scale are also carried out in the workshops and as the particular shop is not known until the very last minute contraband is usually found. It is, however, another matter to pin the blame of ownership on anyone in particular. Searching, taking into account the time of the officers and the hours lost to production, is an expensive business, but, considering the seriousness of men smoking more than a few pennyworth of tobacco a week, it is presumably considered justified. See *drybath; rubdown; Search Book; stiff; snout; safe screw; bent screw*, etc.

Second Division. See *divisions; Criminal Justice Act,* 1948.

sell, to. To sell food or any other commodity for tobacco or 'roll-ups'. To barter. In all prisons there

186

is a constant buying and selling. The following examples give an idea of 'prices' in a modern prison: A *butter* (margarine), a *sugar*, or a *cheese* ration average about one *roll-up* (*q.v.*) each; a *cob and butter* (*q.v.*), two to three roll-ups. Jam pasties, the Sunday bun, or a *duff* cost about two roll-ups each. Many men, *barons* and others, have standing orders with others employed in cookhouse or Officers' Mess. A weekly half-pound packet of margarine may cost from 3*d*. to 6*d*. in cash, or perhaps a quarter of an ounce of tobacco. Cold cooked meat, sausages, rashers of fried bacon can also be obtained regularly for a weekly payment in cash or tobacco.

It is a daily cry in prison, 'Do you want to buy a *sugar*?' Many men never touch their sugar and 'sell' it for 'cash'— in the form of a *roll-up*—as soon as it is issued. Barons and men who take plenty of sugar, buy as much as six or more rations at one meal. They pour it into a little bag, made in the tailors' shop, and carry it in an inside pocket. Although it is strictly prohibited to traffic in any commodity, this small-scale buying and selling is frequently overlooked. If a man buys too much and too openly he immediately puts himself under suspicion. The ever-watchful eye of the hall officer does not miss much. See *snout; buy; roll-up; tailor-made; sugar; butter; cob; Findlay; baron; trafficking.*

shackle up. Tramp's slang. See *drum up.*

shaving. In most prisons shaving is done in cold water only (see *hot water*). Some prisons, however, provide a mug of hot water in the evenings, otherwise shaving is carried out in tea, which is nearly always steaming hot if not strong. Men will go to great lengths to shave regularly, in spite of obstructive rules. In the days of the prison crop shaving was carried out once a week by the prison barber. Men then resorted to numerous devices in order to shave; one was to grind down a piece of broken bottle for use as a razor. A shaven man seen on exercise was promptly taken in for searching, and if any illegal shaving article was found, he was promptly punished with solitary confinement and bread and water. Even to-day the shaving facilities leave much to be desired. See *barber; razor blades*, etc.

shaving-mug. An enamelled mug holding about half a pint is among the standard cell equipment. This mug is used for shaving or as a teeth mug and, by many, for a little extra tea or cocoa when dining in cell and when an 'easy' officer distributes the food.

shaving-soap. A small cube of this commodity is issued quarterly. Owing to the inadequacy of shaving materials it is always saleable. Shaving-soap and razor blades find a ready market, as most men try to keep themselves shaved.

'she.' Frequently used when referring to a homosexual—'She's an untidy bitch.' See *pouff; iron hoof*, etc.

Sheenie. A Jew (*q.v.*).

Sheriff's Fund Committee. Welfare organisation of the Metropolitan Area whose aim is to help prisoners and their families. See *Church Army*.

shirts. Prison shirts are made in the tailors' shops, from material woven at Wakefield. They are of white, with a thin black 'pinstripe'. Theoretically each man has three shirts, the third being 'in the wash'. The rules lay down that after wearing a clean shirt for one week it must be used as a nightshirt for another week. It may then be changed for a clean one and the day shirt kept in its place. Many men try to keep their own shirts by doing their own dhobying. Shirts are a commodity which can always be bought for a cigarette or two; men frequently have the collars altered to fit. Shirts are sometimes bleached until they are almost entirely white. See *bathing kit*, etc.

shoes. In many local prisons shoes issued to prisoners are of all shapes and sizes; many being the first attempts at shoemaking by prisoners. The importance of foot comfort is recognised to a certain extent; special shoes are sometimes made for prisoners on the Medical Officer's authority. Recent purchases of ex-Government footwear have greatly added to foot comfort.

Every prison, if not equipped with a bootshop, has at least some corner where boots and shoes are repaired. Some of the larger prisons have big bootshops and actually make boots for officers and for the police; they also carry out repairs for officers and their families. A small charge is made for this service. See *bootshop*.

Shonk. A Jew (*q.v.*).

shop. Any prison workshop—mailbag shop, tailors', printers', etc.

shop redband. Most prison shops have at least one redband (*q.v.*). In some cases his duty is to keep tally of all piece-work produced, and to help the officer in charge with the clerical work. The shop cleaner is usually a redband whose duties include running messages, and in some prisons each shop has at least one leader. He is kept busy taking parties of men about; the bathing parties are sometimes taken by him to the bath-house and back, or the Governor or Chief Officer may send for a man and the leader can take him from shop to office. See *redband; leader; stage; pay; pay clerk*.

shop, to. To betray; to give a man away; to tell tales which will cause the downfall of another. See *case, to; grass, to*

shop, to. To 'case' a man; to put him on a charge. An officer 'shops' a man when he charges him with some offence. A man put on a charge has been *shopped, cased,* or *done.*

shorthand. One of the many classes run in prison, particularly in the training centres, is a shorthand class, which is a popular subject. See *education; Maidstone.*

shot drill (O). One of several useless tasks given to convicts and prisoners in the 'old days'. Numerous heavy stone 'shots' or cannon balls were placed in a workyard. The unfortunate prisoners were obliged to carry these from one point to another and then back again, until the end of the 'working' day. See *treadmill; gyves; chains,* etc.

Shrewsbury. Local prison with cells for 165. See *Prisons.*

sick book. All men reporting sick are entered in a little book. This is taken to the hospital before 7 a.m. and later returned to the hall from whence it came. The Medical Officer's comments and orders are entered in front of the name of each man reporting sick. This is the landing officer's guide. Men ordered back to work are struck off the list and collected by an officer.

sick, reporting. To report 'sick' a man has to notify the officer who unlocks him in the morning. A printed card, 'R.I.C.' (*q.v.*) or 'M.O.', is then hung on his door handle and, having been given his breakfast, he is locked in until the Medical Officer calls on his rounds. In some prisons this may be as late as 11 or 12 o'clock. In other prisons men have to line up outside a room used by the Medical Officer immediately after breakfast, and then wait until seen.

No matter for what a man reports sick—because he is ill, because he wants permission to see a dentist or oculist—he must remain locked in his cell until the Medical Officer has seen him. The average landing officer feels that if the man were allowed to walk, even as far as the recess after the initial 'slop-out', and anything should happen to him, he is responsible. If the Medical Officer decides the man needs a day in bed he orders him to stay 'R.I.C.'. A card to that effect is hung on his door and once again he is securely locked in. His food is brought from the dining-hall by the duty table cleaner and he does not leave the cell till the next day. A maximum of three days' R.I.C. is allowed, after which a man must be removed to the prison hospital. See *special sick; hospital; diet,* etc.

sick visit. If a man is detained in hospital he is allowed to have his visits there. If, on the other hand, a blood relation is dangerously ill, he may, on Home Office authority, be allowed to visit him or her in hospital. He is given civilian clothes and sent under escort. See *escort.*

sides. The canvas or hessian cut to size for making up the main body of the mailbags. See *mailbags.*

'sir.' Form of address between officers. One officer checking another's party roll will ask, 'All correct, sir?' Prisoners are expected to address members of the prison staff as 'sir'.

skint. Broke (abbreviation for 'skinned').

slabbed and slid. Dead and gone. One who left the prison a long time ago, and who has been forgotten, may be spoken of as being 'slabbed and slid', meaning that he went out long ago and that anything might have happened to him.

slash, to go for a. To visit the urinal. See *karzy*, etc.

slates. An ordinary old-fashioned school slate and pencil is given to each prisoner in the small local prisons and in some of the larger ones. Apart from using the slate for scribbling and drawing on, the prisoner sometimes uses it to indicate to the librarian that he needs a change of books; or to the hall leader that he is in need of salt, soap, etc. See *salt; toothpowder*, etc.

slinger. One who passes counterfeit—'a slush slinger'. See *snide; slush*, etc.

slop. A uniformed policeman. See *bogey*, etc.

slop-out. First order of the day when the cells are unlocked. A man may ring his bell and ask to 'slop-out', but this unpleasant task is usually limited to opening-up time and at 8 p.m., before men are locked in for the night. See *sanitation; open up; slop sink*.

slop sink. There is usually one recess (*q.v.*) to a hall or landing and, apart from a w.c., there is the slop sink which all men on that landing queue up to use at 'slop-out' time. In the older prisons this sink is still a circular basin set in a slab of slate; more up-to-date prisons have the hospital type of sink and it is probable that within a few years there will be some improvement in the present hopelessly inadequate and foul-smelling system of sanitation.

slush. Counterfeit. Forged money. See *slinger; snide; jar*, etc.

smash up. See *bash up; paddy*.

smock. In some prisons overalls or smocks are issued to working parties. The smock buttons at the sleeves and covers the jacket. At one time different coloured collars (of webbing) indicated different grades and stages. For example, men serving life sentences wore red collars. See *bluette, overalls*.

Smoke, the. London or any big city. London is usually referred to as the 'Big Smoke'.

sneakers. Shoes worn by a cat burglar. Any rubber or crepe-soled shoes used when burgling. See *case; drum; screw*, etc.

snide or **Schnide.** Counterfeit coins; faked jewels, etc. Anything in the money or jewel line that is not genuine; *i.e.* snide jars = faked diamonds. See *jar; ice; slush*.

snide, to be. To be cunning. 'He's a "snide" so-and-so' = he's a slippery customer.

snitcher. An informer; a handcuff. See *grasser; darbies*.

snout. Word used collectively to cover all tobacco, hand-rolled and factory-made cigarettes, cigarette ends, and pipe dottles. All prison life centres round tobacco and anything, from food to favours, is obtainable for tobacco.

The word originates from the days when smoking was prohibited in prison. When smoking, the lag cupped his hand and pretended to rub his nose while taking a 'draw' on his cigarette. A warder, seeing a man put his hand to his nose, guessed what he was doing and promptly called him to task. Though this is undoubtedly the correct derivation, it has been suggested that there may be a connection between 'snout' (nose) and 'rhino' (snout or nose). 'Rhino', in slang, refers to money or the weekly pay.

To ask a friend if he has a smoke to spare it is not necessary to speak. A finger laid alongside the nose, an action repeated a hundred times a day in any prison, is all that is necessary.

It is a serious offence for an officer to bring tobacco or other prohibited commodities into prison or to take out letters. Friends visiting a prisoner are liable to prosecution if caught trying to pass money or tobacco, etc.

The efforts of the Howard League for Penal Reform finally persuaded the authorities to permit smoking in prisons (see *pay; lob*). It was then decided that 'by industry and hard work' a man could earn an ounce of tobacco a week and a packet of cigarette papers. With the then top rate of 1s. a week this was possible. A fifty per cent. increase in pay has not brought the present prices into line with prison conditions. The fact that men are allowed to smoke leaves a loophole. Many prisoners and officers, however, are agreed that it would be best to adopt one of two courses. Either prohibit smoking altogether or allow a man to earn (or have sent in) enough tobacco to satisfy the urge. The existing system encourages a man to smoke on 'Snout Day' and for the rest of the week he is thinking out 'fiddles' and selling his food. Furthermore, officers' time costs money, production is held up while searching takes place, and, worst of all, fighting and not infrequently razor slashings occur all through the determination of men to smoke; a harmless enough desire. See *baron; Findlay; buy; sell; tobacco; tobacco substitutes; pay; lob; trafficking; fiddle; rhino*, etc.

snout baron. See *baron; Findlay*.

snout day. Tobacco day. The issue of tobacco is made once a week on whatever day is most convenient to the prison authorities concerned. There is no prison 'shop' or 'canteen', except in rare cases, and the issue is made by an officer who visits the various halls or comes into the workshops with the tobacco. The smallest amount obtainable is usually a quarter of an ounce, which costs 10*d*. This is often shared by two, and even more, men. Tobacco day is, in some prisons, the same day as that on which men are paid. In one convict prison there was a good canteen run by a civilian who visited the prison each Saturday and who had the use of a small store-room into which a counter had been fitted. Here men could buy several brands of tobacco, cigarettes, vinegar (for which they had to provide bottles or jars), coffee, meat extract, and a variety of similar commodities. At this prison there were convicts earning, with stage pay (*q.v.*), as much as 2*s*. 6*d*. a week. See *snout; pay*, etc.

snow. Cocaine (from its appearance). See *dope*.

snow. Silver. Silver coins or silver articles. See *white; arge; pewter; pony in white*.

snow-dropping. Stealing washing from clothes lines. See also *drumming; buzzing; whizzing*.

soap. Washing soap (yellow) is issued once a week, either from the P.W.S. (*q.v.*) on collecting clean clothing, in the bath-house, or by the hall leader, who puts each ration in the cells. A few prisons allow a little carbolic soap for scrubbing, but this privilege is rare. Soap in any quantity is always available, at a price, and is one of the commodities most frequently 'bought' by officers. See *shaving; hot water; sell; buy*, etc.

soup. Nitro-glycerine. Used for blowing safes. See also *jelly; Peterman; screwsman*.

sparklers (O). Word once used for diamonds, which to-day are mostly referred to as *ice* (*q.v.*).

sparsie. Sixpence. See *spratt; half a chip*.

Special. A convict who is on 'Special' stage. He reaches this after four years and wears a grey band on the sleeves of his coat (see *bluecoat*). Extra privileges are allowed him, such as an extra hour's recreation in the evening and the use of a gas ring in the 'Specials' Room', where he can 'brew up'. He may also have newspapers sent in. See *stage; greyband*, etc.

special bath. As distinct from an 'ordinary bath'. Used for delousing, etc. See *one ordinary bath*.

special letter. In addition to the regulation letters a man may apply to the Governor for an extra letter, providing he has a good reason for doing so. See *letters; applications, Governor's; reception letter; Christmas letter*.

special release. Spoken of as a 'Special'. (See *court martial; blue papers*.) 'Special Releases' are very rare among men sentenced by the civil courts but quite common among court-martial cases. Men granted a 'Special' generally have a sudden and unexpected 'call-up' and are out of the prison within an hour or so. The Governor is sometimes told by telephone that a certain man has been granted a 'Special', but the man cannot be released until instructions come through in writing. See *lifer*.

special sick. Men intending to report sick must do so at unlocking time (about 6.40 a.m.). If, however, a man is taken ill he may report 'special sick' at any hour of the day or night. A man who reports special sick is taken either to his cell, where he is locked in pending a visit from the Medical Officer or a Hospital Officer, or he is taken direct to the Hospital. Men sometimes go special sick in order to avoid some unpleasant task, or to get out of a jam after an altercation with an officer. This is somewhat risky, for frivolous behaviour is duly rewarded with three days' bread and water. See *sick; R.I.C.; hospital; M.O.*

spiel. Sales talk. 'He shot his spiel to the boys' = he told them the 'old story'. See *ackamaraka; spieler; boracic*.

spieler. One whose job is to attract custom to booths— at fairs, circuses, etc.—by standing outside shouting the attractions.

Also, an officer who likes the sound of his own voice. An officer who is always shouting out instructions or reading notices aloud in halls and workshops. See *screw; caser*, etc.

spin, a. A cab rank. Authorised taxi stand.

spiv. Until popularised by the press 'spiv' was an everyday word in prison talk. To-day it seems to have lost favour and in some prisons is never heard. A 'spiv' is one who dresses loudly, padded shoulders and jazzy tie, etc., and who lives by his wits. Among numerous suggestions as to the origin of the word are the following:

Back slang for V.I.P.'s (Very Important Persons).

From the Police records of 'Suspected Persons and Itinerant Vagrants'.

By far the most likely derivation is that it is of Romany origin. In the seventeenth century reference is made to the town of Newmarket being full of 'spivics'. Spivic is still used in the Newmarket district as an onomatopœic synonym for sparrow. The Romanies used the word as a term of contempt for those who followed them around picking up the leavings.

Another source quotes the 'spiv' as being one who travels from one race meeting to another taking care of horses due to run in the following race. After the race they walk them round to cool off, sponge them down, and generally attend to their welfare. If this is the true origin then it seems unfair that one who earns an honest living should give name to idlers and cheats.

Another source quotes a 'spiv' as one who obtains a living without having to work for it and adds that the word has been in use in Newmarket for a decade or more, with this meaning.

A medical psychologist's description of a 'spiv', quoted in the *Daily Telegraph*, is perhaps the perfect definition: '. . . a common type of individual who combined in himself an inflated ego, a rather "pansoid" tendency to exhibitionism and self display and an incorrigible and incurable determination to avoid work, whatever the trouble or inconvenience to himself or others . . . his intelligence is brightish but never high; he is always sure that he will get away with what better brains would tell him he cannot—in the long run . . . his natural symbol and coat of arms is the fiddle.' See *baron; barrow boy; drone; wide boy; actor*, etc.

split (M). Refers to a detective. *Bogey* (*q.v.*) is the more common word. Also, to share; to divide up the loot.

sports. Football is by far the most popular game played in prison, even though the pitch is often only the asphalt parade ground. The large prisons usually have a grass field and some convict prisons have spacious grasslands where two games can be played at the same time. Football is followed enthusiastically and inter-house games usually carry a great deal of money and tobacco on the result.

Cricket has quite a good following and is played in season, limited only by the space available.

When there were Americans and Canadians from the forces in our prisons, it naturally followed that baseball and softball would be played. The popularity of these games, however, soon waned with the departure of the 'foreigners'. Volley-ball, basket-ball, and hockey are also played in some prisons, but no game equals the popularity of football. Cricket is a good second. League football is followed and bets are laid on outside games (see *gambling*). The average standard of sportsmanship is poor and it is no uncommon thing for men to boo their own hall team for the most trivial of reasons. See *Sports Day*.

Sports Day. About twice a year, at Whitsun and on August Bank Holiday, many prisons hold a Sports

Day, with prizes of cigarettes and tobacco for the winners. A Sports Committee is selected by the prisoners, who choose hall representatives. Officers and non-uniformed staff help to make Sports Days a success and often subscribe towards the prizes. Unfortunately the efforts of the staff are not always appreciated and, as with football and other games, the sportsmanship displayed is, on the whole, poor.

Most programmes include the 66 yards dash, 100 yards, 220 yards, and the half-mile. High and long jumps are popular and occasionally there is the mile, a distance found to be rather too gruelling. Relay races and other events between halls rouse enthusiasm and the obstacle and 'old clothes' races provide amusement. See *sports*.

'spot.' Young prisoner or young convict in a local prison, where he wears a distinguishing circle sewn to the upper part of his sleeves. See *Y.P.; Y.C.; badge*, etc.

spratt. Sixpence. See *sparsie; half a chip*, etc.

spray-painting. Some products from prison shops require spraying before being sent out. Men engaged on spray-painting are entitled to a pint of milk a day. They frequently sell half or all this. Articles sprayed include metal containers, tool and machine boxes, shelves, mat frames, etc. See also *printers'; shop; tinshop*.

spring beds. See *beds, spring*.

squawk. A petition. Sometimes refers to an appeal. See *petition; scream; bleat*.

squeak or **squeal** (R). To tell tales; to give another man away. This word is rarely used in prison; the most popular word being *grass* (*q.v.*). See *grasser*,

199

squealer or **squeaker** (R). One who cannot be trusted with any information, a 'grasser'.

squealer, the. The police radio car. See *Sweeney*.

staff. The prison staff comprises Governor, Deputy Governor, Assistant Governor(s), Steward and clerical staff, on the non-uniformed side. Chief Officer, two or more Principal Officers, tradesmen officers and disciplinary officers, Engineer, Cook, and Hospital Officers on the uniformed side. Porters and some night officers do not wear uniform and may be part-timers. Chaplain and Medical Officer do not, of course, wear uniform and there is usually one D.P.A. (*q.v.*) representative, but he is not on the prison staff. Civilian instructors are employed in many prisons. See *clerical staff; Governor's clerk; steward; gate screw; night screw; censor; prison officer*, etc.

staff college. A series of training courses for new prison officers is held at Wakefield. See *Imperial Training College*.

Stafford. Local prison with accommodation for 681. See *Prisons*.

stage. The system of 'stages' is disappearing and all men, on reception into prison, are given equal privileges which they can lose by misconduct. In some prisons, and particularly in the convict prisons, the stage system is still in force. In local prisons men 'come on stage' after a few weeks, and are then entitled to such privileges as dining in association or attending concerts, etc. In convict prisons there has, as yet, been no modification in the old system. During the first 18 months the prisoner wears grey and his privileges are limited, though usually he may go to concerts, lectures, etc. At 18 months he 'comes on stage', the First Stage, and is given a black band to wear on each sleeve. At two and a half years he changes his grey coat for a blue one, and on reaching the Special Stage (*q.v.*), at four years, wears grey bands on his sleeves.

Until the beginning of the late war stage progress was marked by a certain number of marks awarded daily. These could be docked by any officer and were recorded on a special card fixed in the wooden holder outside each cell. This holder also held the 'cell card' (*q.v.*). Although the mark system is no longer met with, instruction cards for display in cell are still being printed (No. 144). Cell boards are also still being made several sizes larger than necessary, with space for the 'stage card'. In view of the general trend of prisons and the attitude of the Prison Commissioners towards a new system, it is highly improbable that this old stage marking system will ever be used again. See *stage pay* (below) ; *greyband; bluecoat*, etc.

stage pay. In convict prisons the system of payment by stages is still in force. In addition to the weekly pay in the workshops there is an allowance of 2*d.* a week for each year served. A man reaching the First Stage (18 months) qualifies for this and the stage pay increases by the same rate with each successive stage reached. There is a maximum sum which, according to the printed rules, may be earned. This is stated to be 5*s.*, but earnings of 3*s.* are rare. See *stage; pay; lob*.

stairs, up the. The Assize Court. See *Follies*.

'stand by your doors.' The familiar cry of officers when the men come into the halls and, before locking them up, it is required to check either the number of men or certain cell articles. In the event of a suspected escape men are usually marched into their halls and stand in front of their cell doors, so that unoccupied cells can be seen at a glance. See *banged up; have it away; tally*, etc.

Standing Orders. The Book of Rules by which the prisons are run, the 'K.R.'s' of the Prison Service. Prisoners have no access to this, but when charged with an offence it is explained to them before sentencing.

Stanwell. A site purchased for a women's prison and girls' Borstal Institution and which is now farmed by 'boys' from Feltham Borstal Institution. See *Borstal Institutions; Prisons*, etc.

star. A 'star' prisoner is usually, though not necessarily, a first offender and as such is segregated from the more hardened and habitual offenders. Various prisons for both ordinary prisoners and convicts are reserved for 'stars'. See *Maidstone; Ley Hill; Aldington Camp; training centre*, etc.

starch (M) or **starched collar** (R). A 'stiff', or illegal letter. Also, *birds of a feather*.

statistics. See *Report, Commissioners'*. This report deals fully with the authorised statistics relating to crime and punishment.

steam tug. Mug.

steamer. A 'mug' (rhyming slang from steam tug—mug). A beggar, on receiving a 'mean' tip from some soft-hearted stranger, would refer to him as a 'cheese-cake steamer' (R).

stencils. The last stage in the manufacture of Post Office mailbags is the stencilling of Government marks. A large metal stencil is used and marking ink is applied with an old shaving brush. This somewhat messy job is greatly enjoyed by the average prisoner engaged on the task. See *mailbags*.

steward. An important member of the non-uniformed branch of the Prison Service. He is responsible for all purchases for the prison, maintenance of stock, food, furniture, and general equipment, etc. He has his office in the administration block and has little or no contact with the prisoners. See *staff; prison officer; clerical staff*, etc.

stick. Jemmy. Usually made of a length of high-grade steel, about 18 in. long. See *stripping*. Also, *cane*.

stiff. An illegal letter sent out of or smuggled into prison. These are usually taken out by 'bent screws'—dishonest officers—either for a cash payment or as a favour. Illegal letters are written for two purposes. The majority are on matters concerning money and tobacco to be smuggled in (see *screw, bent; snout*, etc.). Others are written by those men whose 'love letters', to wife or girl friend, are such that he does not want the official censor to read them. See *Joey; censor; special letter; starch; love letters*. Also, a corpse. Anyone who has been knocked out, either in a fight or by accident.

stir (R). Prison. Used occasionally by the older men and by those who are serving a first sentence. From the Romany 'sturiben', which derives from the verb 'to confine'.

stocktaking. Periodical check-up on articles of clothing and cell equipment. During stocktaking all men are sent back to their cells while the officers go round to each one in turn. The usual practice is to take certain articles on different days. Thus one day a check might be on towels, belts, and socks. The officer asks each prisoner how many of these articles he has. The prisoner answers 'one of each', because he might get into trouble if he had more. This business usually occupies about two hours, and as it is conducted during working hours, there is a heavy loss in working time. Stocktaking in the shops means the closing down of each shop for anything from half a day to two days. During this time the men are divided into parties and found odd jobs, such as digging or scrubbing. See *search; P.W.S.*, etc.

stokehole. The boiler-house where steam is generated for heating, cooking, and bathing. The chief stoker is usually a civilian and he is assisted by at least one prisoner, usually a seaman by trade. See *boiler-house; heating.*

strait-jacket. See *restraints; darbies; cape*, etc.

stretch. A stretch equals one year's imprisonment. 'Two stretch(es)'—two years. Although, strictly speaking, a sentence of three years and upwards constitutes penal servitude, such sentences are frequently spoken of as 'a four stretch' or a 'five stretch', etc. See *time; lagging; P.S.; 'imp'; lifer*, etc.

stripping. The process of opening a safe with the *stick* (also *cane*), or *jemmy*. This can be a long process and the use of *jelly* (gelignite) is more popular. It is first necessary to find a crack into which the jemmy can be wedged and with the modern safe this is improbable.

strong cell. See *box; paddy.*

study hour. In some prisons the hour between 6 and 7 p.m. is reserved for study. Men are sent to their cells and are not allowed to talk or to move about. Cell doors are open and a man may not leave his cell, even for the recess visit, except by permission from the hall or landing officer to, 'Fall out, sir'. Every facility is granted for private study and correspondence courses (*q.v.*) in the 'modern' prisons and training centres. See *education; Maidstone*, etc.

stumer. Cheque or bank draft. Unlike banknotes, which are easily changed, a 'stumer' is a dead loss to the burglar. As a rule cheques, etc., are left behind, only banknotes and cash being considered worth taking. Also, a forged cheque; worthless promissory note.

stumer, to drop a. To make a mistake. A 'stumer' = a mistake.

Sudbury. Recently opened prison camp near Nottingham. See *Prisons; open-camp prisons*.

sugar, a. The measure of West-Indian brown sugar, in a small tin, issued each evening to prisoners. It is used extensively for bartering. One *sugar* is worth approximately one *snout* or *roll-up*. See *buy; sell; butter; trafficking*, etc.

suicide. Suicide is strongly discouraged in all prisons. Knives, razor blades, needles, and any other article which might be of help to a miserable soul seeking escape are carefully controlled according to the type of prison and its inmates. Electricity is stepped-down to about 50 volts for most cells lights. A man cannot thus attempt to electrocute himself, though, should he think of it, the bulb may be removed and taken in powdered form. Razor blades and knives are not allowed in many cells, but there is still glass from the window to provide a means for slashing arteries. Many men swallow needles, buttons, etc., in an attempt to escape from the consequences of often trivial offences, such as stealing bicycles, odd articles of clothing, etc. Such attempts are pathetic, in that they are made by men who are not criminals but who have 'made a slip'. Netting (see *safety net*) across the landings prevents jumping from the top floors; ropes, ties, belts are taken from likely suicides and other precautions are rigidly followed. See *executions*.

supper. The last meal of the day, sometimes called 'tea', is at 5 p.m. This comprises a pint of tea, a 'cob and butter' (*q.v.*), and a sugar ration. Some prisons give some little extra, such as a couple of onions, a cheese and potato spread, etc. Until October 1947 a pint of cocoa was issued with this meal. Cocoa is now issued at 8 p.m. and tea substituted at 'supper'. See *cocoa, evening; menu*, etc.

sus. Suspicion. 'He was arrested on sus.' A 'sus' = a suspect.

Swansea. Local prison with accommodation for 161 men in cells. See *Prisons*.

Sweeney. The police radio van (from rhyming slang, Sweeney Todd—squad, squad car). Also, *squealer; holler wagon*, etc.

sweets. For the benefit of non-smokers many prisons make sweets available to prisoners. Usually they are ordered in advance, the hall leader recording requirements in the 'Sweet Book'. This book, together with the tobacco book, is handed in to the pay clerk, who informs the authorities of the amounts required for the week. See *shop; snout*, etc.

swill. All waste food is placed in bins, which are collected daily by a local pig farmer. Where swill can be used on the prison farms it is carted by men working on the prison farm party. See *diet*, etc.

swinging the line. Passing books, tobacco, messages from one cell to another by means of a length of line (usually thread from the mailbag shop). This can only be done by a man in a cell above or next to another. The window opening usually measures about 6 in. by 4 in. and is some 7 ft. from the floor. The man stands on his chair, pushes his book or message out of the window, and lowers it on the line. He cannot see down, but by swinging it backwards and forwards and working up a momentum it can be grabbed by a man in a lower cell or in the next cell. Although this practice is common it is always open to apprehension and is duly punished. See *love letters*, etc.

swordsman. A fence. One who receives stolen property. See *fence; granny*.

synagogue. Most prisons have at least a small room or converted cell set aside for use of Jewish prisoners. See *Jew; religion*.

T

tab. Ear. Also, *lug*.

tab. Ringed tabs, made of hessian or canvas are sewn to completed mailbags as a separate operation. These tabs are usually made by men on piece-work and sewn on by others. See *mailbags*, etc.

tabbing. The process of sewing on tabs. See above, and *cell task*, etc.

table, cell. A small wood or slate table is fixed permanently into the wall in the corner of each cell and next to the door. See *table, study; cell; lighting*, etc.

table leader. In those prisons where men are allowed to associate a leader (*q.v.*) is put in charge of each table of about a dozen men. He is responsible for the collection and distribution of food and for the tidiness of the table and surrounding floor space. The table orderly for the day goes with the leader when collecting or returning food pails. See below, also, *association*.

table marks. The officer in charge of the dining-hall inspects all tables at meal-times. Marks for tidiness are usually allotted daily and slackness on the part of table leader or orderly results in loss of marks. At the end of each month the table with the most marks is awarded a small tobacco prize, which is divided between men on that table.

table orderly. Each man at a table takes his turn to act as orderly (see *table leader*). Frequently one man, at least, is willing to have this job as a permanency and receives payment of a penny a week from each of the others. This gives a good income, and where two or more men wish for the job on one table it is taken in turn, each doing a week at a time. Officers shut an eye to this practice, which is officially not allowed.

table, study. Men engaged on private study, such as correspondence courses (*q.v.*), are allowed a small unpainted wooden table. In a few prisons these are standard issue in all cells. Although it is, strictly speaking, against all rules to stain these tables, men do so and maintain them with a high polish. See *cell; furniture, cell*, etc.

tailor-made. A factory-made cigarette. In prison these have an enhanced value, though only the *barons* (*q.v.*) can afford to smoke them. Normally each one is broken up and re-rolled into two, three, and even four thin little cigarettes or *roll-ups*, which are used for trading. Most men have a taste, or soon acquire one, for dark tobacco, but there are always a few 'smokers of discernment' who prefer an occasional cigarette of a recognised brand. Therefore it is always possible to 'sell' a tailor-made for, as a rule, two *roll-ups* of dark tobacco. See *snout; tobacco substitutes; roll-up*, etc.

tailors' shop. In these shops all prison garments are made and repaired. The bigger shops handle outside contracts for various Government departments. These include such things as pockets for battle-dresses, hussifs, holdalls. The end of the war terminated many contracts, but other articles include sea cadets' uniforms, officers' garments, etc.

Men working in tailors' shops have their own *fiddles*, which include belt-making for those who dislike the thin prison belt of hessian. Poachers' pockets, sugar bags, money bags, etc., are also recognised articles for 'sale' to other prisoners. New collars can be attached to shirts; trousers and coats pressed or altered are among the services available to the prisoner who has the tobacco with which to pay. Socks, mostly made in these shops, can usually be obtained new for two roll-ups. See also *labour; buy; sell; fiddle; trafficking.*

take a powder. To desert; to run away (service). Also, *trot, on the.*

talking. It is common belief that prisoners are not allowed to talk; that all convicts mutter from the corner of their mouths, even years after discharge. A man on remand is not allowed to talk and this is for his own good. Were free conversation allowed there is the possibility that he might give away something that would be detrimental to his chances at his trial. In theory, however, this sounds easy; in practice, where it is inevitable for men to meet, conversations are carried on at all times—on the exercise yards when a man's back is turned towards the guard and he can speak just loudly enough for the man behind to hear; in chapel, particularly during hymn-singing; and at odd moments when all are waiting their turn to 'slop-out'.

Among convicted prisoners there is no restriction on talking, though in theory it is not allowed in the work-shops. Providing it does not hinder work, however, it is usually overlooked, but in the 'bad' prisons it gives the warders an excuse to 'case' any man they do not like the look of. See *association.*

tally. The parade at which prisoners are counted. This takes place before or after morning exercise, before and after the dinner hour, and after labour in the evening. Men are also counted before being unlocked and at locking-up time, when both day and night watch check the figures.

Also, the point at which men 'march past' for the purpose of being counted. The Orderly Officer or a Principal Officer usually stands at this point, either alone or with an assistant, writing on a little slate 'pad' the number of men on each party. To the total of this he adds those who are sick in their cells or on some special job. There is a very rigid rule regarding punctuality and attendance at tally.

tapeworm. The Chief Officer; sometimes a Principal Officer (because of the amount of braid sewn on coat and trousers). See *corned beef; screwdriver; P.O.*

tapped signals. There is a common belief that when prisoners are locked in their cells there is an incessant underground 'buzz' of messages and signals passing from cell to cell. Although two men may occasionally arrange some signal to be given if a certain 'fiddle' is successfully concluded, there is no regular code of signals and conversations by such means are virtually nil. See *quadratic alphabet.*

tart. The original meaning of this word is unknown to most prisoners and it is loosely applied when speaking of any girl or woman. Also, *bride; Brahma; Richard; Jane; brass; half-brass; mystery; fluff,* etc.

tart, ritzy. 'Classy.' Any girl of the upper or middle classes. Any girl who dresses well or who speaks with an educated voice.

T.B. cells. A number of cells on an upper landing are set aside for cases of T.B. which are not serious enough for hospital. These have special windows which, while maintaining security by means of stout bars, can be thrown open to allow a maximum of fresh air. Generally there is a fixed hinged bed with a spring frame. See *isolation cells.*

T.B. library. T.B. patients are not allowed to handle books from the prison library. Books are kept apart for their use and the T.B. library is usually located in a disused cell. See also *scabies; V.D. cells.*

tea. See *supper.*

tea-leaf. The Chief Officer (rhyming slang). See *tapeworm*, etc. Also, a thief (rhyming slang).

tearaway. One who resorts to violence at the slightest excuse. Usually a coward who climbs down when opposition is encountered. See also *bash up*, etc.

telephones. See *blower.*

temporary duty. Officers are liable to serve a period of about two months at a time on temporary duty at another prison and a roster is made out for this. Other temporary duty for which a prison officer may be summoned is that of C.C. (Condemned Cell) Duty. See *C.C.; death watch.*

theatricals. Particularly in convict prisons, where there is also more time to prepare, are found enthusiastic amateur actors. Some plays put on by prisons are of a surprisingly high standard. Local prisons usually manage to put on variety shows and several prisons have managed their own pantomimes. See *concerts; amusements*, etc.

thread. The coarse string used for sewing mailbags. This is issued in skeins and, when required, is wound round the legs of a chair and then cut at one point to give identical lengths. It is then waxed by hand. It can be used for various illegal purposes: to weave into a rope for escape, to swing messages from one cell to another, or to play with in the long evenings. See *mailbags; amusements; swinging the line; waxing.*

ticket (O). The 'ticket of leave' is an obsolete term for the *licence* (*q.v.*) issued to convicts on discharge. The Criminal Justice Act, 1948, has abolished the 'ticket' and introduced a modified form of reporting to the police, etc.

tickler, the. The cat-o'-nine-tails. See *cat; get your back scratched; apron; corporal punishment.*

time. To 'do time', or 'bird' (*q.v.*). To serve a sentence of imprisonment. Sentences up to three years are referred to as imprisonment, or 'imp' for short. Three years and upwards are spoken of as a 'lagging', or penal servitude (see *stretch; lagging*). All sentences are referred to in slang. A short sentence is spoken of as a 'haircut' or 'week-end'. The conception of a short sentence depends on the type of prison. A month's 'imp' in a local prison is short, whereas in a convict prison a 'three-year man' dare not open his mouth in complaint when his companions may be doing anything from five years to life.

The following serve as examples:

1 month	A 'moon', a 'woodener' ('moon' is the most common expression).
2 months	Two moon.
3 ,,	A carpet.
4 ,,	Four moon, etc.
6 ,,	Half a stretch.
9 ,,	Nine moon.
12 ,,	A stretch, occasionally called a 'leggner' (*i.e.* to stretch 'a leg').
18 ,,	A stretch and a half.
21 ,,	A pontoon (from the card game).
2 years	A two stretch.
3 ,, and above	A 'lagging'.
4 ,,	A 'lagging' or a 'rofe' (pron. 'roaf').
5 ,,	A 'lagging' or 'handful' or 'flim'.

Other sentences are spoken of as, 'A seven or a ten stretch', etc. See under separate headings. Also, *lifer; H.M.P.*

time recorder. Throughout the prison are keys for the time-recording clocks issued to the night watch. The cards from these machines are changed by the Principal Officer in the morning and the marked cards, duly entered on a special form, are passed to the Governor for his signature.

Short-term prisoners mark off the days by many different means. The most common, of course, is to cross off each one on a calendar, but where these are not permitted marks are scratched in some inconspicuous place on the wall, or in the slate floor just behind the door. Men serving long sentences soon tire of this pastime.

time-table. Roughly speaking, there are two time-tables in prison. Those prisons where there is a shortage of staff and work for men to do lock the prisoners up for most of the day. In other prisons where things are run on a more up-to-date system, most of the prisoners' time is spent in the workshops or on classes. Individual halls issue time-tables in these latter establishments, but in general they must conform to the routine of the prison. The following is taken from a hall in a modern training centre:

6.15 a.m.	*First Bell.*	All men will rise, make up beds, and clean cells before 6.45 a.m.
6.45 ,,		Doors unlocked. All men slop-out. After this all men will return to their cells and remain there, *except* table leaders and orderlies, who will prepare tables for breakfast.
6.55 ,,		*Breakfast Bell.* All men go to tables. No one to use recess (*q.v.*).

7.15 a.m.	*Bell.*	Men may leave tables and smoke, *not* before, and may go upstairs or to recess.
7.25	,,	Table leaders and orderlies tidy tables.
7.30	,,	*Bell.* All men form up on ground floor for exercise.
8.00	,,	Parade for work. March-off tally.
11.50	,,	Return from work. All men to cells, except leaders and orderlies, who will prepare for dinner.
11.55	,,	*Dinner Bell.* Sit down to tables.
12.15 p.m.	*Bell.*	Men may leave tables and smoke; may visit cell and recess, etc.
12.40	,,	*Bell.* Form up on ground floor ready for exercise.
1.00	,,	Parade for work.
4.50	,,	Return from work. All men to cells except table leaders and orderlies, who will prepare tables for tea.
4.55	,,	*Tea Bell.* Sit down to tables.
5.15	,,	*Bell.* May leave table and smoke, visit cell and recess.
5.25	,,	*Bell.* All men will go to ground floor association. Early classes to stand by.

N.B. Between 5.25 and 6.35 p.m. bells no man will be on upper floors without duty officer's permission and for a specific reason (e.g. study, letter-writing, etc.).

5.30 p.m.	1st Classes ⎫	
6.00 ,,	2nd ,, ⎬ summoned by bells.	
6.30 ,,	3rd ,, ⎭	
6.35 ,,	*Bell.* Clear hall, all men not on classes to cells.
7.00 ,,	Leaders not on duty may use Leaders' Room.
8.00 ,,	*Bell.* Beds down. Cocoa.
9.00 ,,	All leaders, etc., to cells.

Week-end time-tables are modified to fit in with football on Saturdays, chapel on Sundays, etc.

In local prisons where there is no association and labour hours (*q.v.*) are short, all men are locked in by 5 p.m.

tinder. Scorched rag for use with tinder box and flint (see *flint*). Tinder is made by burning rag, preferably very old rag or linen, and then smothering it with a tin or by closing it in a box before it burns away. When cold it is kept in the tinder box.

tinder box. Throughout the prisons the tinder box is the recognised means of obtaining a light for a cigarette. Although illegal in most prisons the carrying of boxes is usually overlooked. Some men use any small tin, others have special ones made in tinshop or carpenters'. In the case of wooden tinder boxes, small coffin-shaped ones are most popular. The box contains scorched rag, a piece of razor blade, and a flint wedged into a small piece of wood, generally an inch or so cut off a prison pen. To obtain a light the razor blade is struck against the flint, the spark falling on the tinder. Pipe-smokers place a small piece of tinder across the bowl of the pipe and then ignite it with the flint. As soon as a light has been obtained the lid of the box is closed and the tinder will last quite a while. See *flints; chipper*, etc.

tinshop. Prison tinshops turn out articles for Government departments as well as for the prisons. Such articles include sugar tins, tin knives, paraffin cans, canisters, and tin trays. The larger shops also have welding facilities, where men may learn this trade, also spray-painting shops. See *welding; spray-painting; manufacturing stores*, etc.

tobacco. In all prisons tobacco is referred to as *snout* (*q.v.*), and a finger laid silently along the side of the nose asks for a smoke.

tobacco book. Men able to buy tobacco give their names in to hall or table leader. Their requirements are recorded in a book which is handed to the pay clerk at the end of the week. This book also serves as a part check on the amount spent by any one man.

tobacco, home-grown. In a few prisons the odd tobacco plant, possibly hidden behind a screen of Michaelmas daisies, is carefully tended and finally dried off and smoked. An experiment, in one prison, to grow a plot of tobacco for equal distribution failed because pilferers could not leave the plants to grow to proper size. That which was harvested and cured made an excellent smoke.

tobacco substitutes. The average prisoner, having been allowed just enough tobacco to whet his appetite, soon resorts to substitutes. The list of things smoked by men 'dying for a cigarette' would fill many pages. Naturally, substitutes depend on the type of prison. The fortress-like 'local', with only a bare concrete exercise yard and one flower-bed, offers a poor comparison with a prison where flowers are cultivated and where men work in field and garden.

Herbalists' 'smoking mixtures' have been sold in some prisons (see *herbs*), but, say many, why pay for a substitute when it is to be had for nothing? Men have been known to smoke coir from the prison mattress, rolled up brown paper—reminiscent of childhood's early attempts to smoke—and dried tea-leaves filched from the garbage pail. Tea leaves, if fresh and consequently marketable for real tobacco, can be smoked without burning the lips or throat. Dried iris leaves, filched from an autumn or winter bed, can taste rather like a mild tobacco. Coltsfoot, clover, walnut leaves, chrysanthemum leaves and seed, or the dried flower are also smokable. Where possible the smoker mixes his substitute with tobacco, but frequently this is impossible and by sticking to one substitute he is able to acquire a taste for it. Hollyhocks, walnut leaves, or wild clematis all burn best in a pipe, but to the desperate man anything to which fire can be set is considered worth trying. See *snout*.

toilet paper. Proper toilet paper is supplied. In prisons where men have access to the lavatories it is put in each compartment. In other prisons it is issued individually by hall cleaners. See *karzy*, etc.

toke (O). Once popular name for bread. See *cob*.

ton. One hundred pounds sterling. See also *century; monkey; pony; flim; crackle*, etc.

toothpowder. If not issued to each cell, toothpowder is placed in a large box on a table in the hall, together with boxes of salt and Epsom salts. Men may then help themselves. Proprietary brands of toothpaste and tooth-powders are frequently smuggled into prison, but men in possession of such are liable to punishment.

top step, on the. 'He's standing on the top step.' Said of a man standing trial; this means that there is every prospect of his being given the maximum sentence.

top, to. To hang. *Topped*, hanged. *Top and chop*, which means the same thing, probably dates from the days when the executioner wielded an axe and public executions were popular. See *executions*.

topping shed. Execution shed or room. See *executions*.

Tortworth Court. Convict prison near Bristol. See *Ley Hill*, by which name it is now known.

tosh. A 'bloke'. The same as 'mush' or 'moosh' and words of equal popularity. Also a form of greeting, 'Wotcher, tosh?' See *jockey*.

tosheroon. Half a crown. See *bed and breakfast*.

tot. Small porcelain measure for medicines. See *hospital; M.O.*, etc.

touched. Arrested (from the touch on the arm by a detective about to arrest a man). Also, *get your collar felt.*

trade assistant. See *tradesman officer*. An officer whose main duties are not of a disciplinary nature. Abbreviated to 'T.A.'.

trades. See *vocational training*. All prisoners, except those serving very short sentences, have a chance to learn a trade of some sort. Apart from the three vocational courses encouraged by the Commission, a man can learn something about painting, bricklaying, tailoring on machines, welding, the work of a tinsmith, and general agriculture and gardening. Help is sometimes given to a man, if he shows keenness, to find suitable employment on discharge. See *education; D.P.A.*

tradesman officer. Prison officers are divided into tradesmen and disciplinary officers. The former are qualified in some trade or other, such as that of electrician, plumber, bricklayer, etc. See *prison officer*.

trafficking. Any dealing in forbidden articles. Tobacco, money, and illegal letters are the principal mediums for encouraging trafficking. Other articles include such things as proprietary brands of toothpaste, toothpowder, haircream, nail-scissors and nailfiles; sweets, chocolate and cakes, meat extract and cubes, and a large variety of small luxuries which some prisoners will strive to get. Trafficking is punishable by dismissal and imprisonment for officers and by loss of remission (the same thing as imprisonment) and bread and water, etc., for a prisoner. Friends of a prisoner who help in trying to smuggle any article into a prison are also liable to prosecution and imprisonment. See *baron; snout*, etc.

training centre. A new system in the treatment of offenders was first tried out at Wakefield Prison, in Yorkshire. This included a fairly extensive educational scheme and an 'open' camp in the country. The system was later extended to Maidstone, where it was intensified and moulded into one that is now looked on, by the Prison Commission and others, as the standard for the future. The system at Maidstone is to be adopted at Wakefield and it is also proposed to extend the system of regional training centres to cover the whole country. Another centre is to be opened for the south-west region and Chelmsford (*q.v.*) will also be run on similar lines.

The idea of 'training', as the governing principle of prison regime, has developed over the last 20 years. The principle being now agreed on, it is the method which has to be defined. Men will be classified as 'trainable' and 'non-trainable', and those serving short sentences (for this purpose a short sentence is up to four years) will be sent to the establishment considered most suitable. Women will be dealt with separately (see *women's prisons*) and long-sentence prisoners will constitute another category. Persistent offenders will come under separate consideration and the whole question of such individuals is looked at in a new light. See *Maidstone; recidivist; Criminal Justice Act*, 1948; *Y.P.*, etc.

tramp's lagging. Three months' imprisonment. Tramps usually get a week or two at a time for vagrancy. Three months, therefore, is considered severe. See *beggar's lagging; time*.

trot, on the. A fugitive from the services or from the police. 'On the run.' See also *trotter; take a powder*.

trotter. A deserter. One who is wanted by the police.

trustie. In the 'old days' a privileged prisoner was called a 'trustie'. He was allowed a certain amount of freedom of movement about the prison and was given the pick of the jobs, such as cleaning the officers' lavatory, etc. To-day the 'trustie', or 'redcollar', has become leader or redband. See *stage; leader; redband; special*, etc.

tube (M). Officer who listens to information given by 'squealers'; a 'screw' who listens to a 'bubble' (or rumour). 'To put the bubble in the tube' is to give information to those in authority, in the knowledge that it will get someone into trouble. See *bubble; grass; screw*, etc.

turnover. A personal search or a cell search, or both together. 'A thorough turnover' a thorough search, leaving nothing untouched. See also *drybath; search, routine.*

twirl. Prison officer. Word second in popularity to 'screw'. Originating from the days when the warder carried the keys (or twirls) on a large ring. See *screw; bent twirl*, etc.

twirls. Keys, particularly skeleton keys. These consist usually of pieces of strong wire of varying thickness, with a right-angle bend. A loop in the centre of the 'stem' allows pressure to be exerted while feeling for the ward or for the right amount of bend to use. The stem of such a key is, in appearance, rather like a Rugby-Pelham bit. See *keys*, etc.

U

unchubb or **unmiln.** To unlock. (From Chubb and Miln, well-known safe and lock makers.) See also *chubbed in; banged in; milned in.*

underwear. Summer underwear consists of coarse 'drawers', which hang halfway down the shins, and cotton vests. The grey flannel winter underwear is slowly being replaced by purchases of ex-Government stocks. The old grey vest and drawers were the cause of much merriment. The drawers were supplied with tapes for tying below the knees. The new issues are of good quality but shortages make it necessary to limit long woollen pants to men over 35 or 40 and woollen vests are, in some prisons, issued only on Medical Officer's authority. See *bathing kit*.

uniform. In 1949 a newly designed uniform was issued to prisoners. Whereas the earlier uniform comprised a thick grey jacket with one pocket and trousers of a 'moleskin' material, the new uniform has, in addition to the breast pocket, two side pockets. This has obviated the necessity for wearing illegal 'poacher's pockets' inside the jacket. The trousers are now made of the same material as the jacket and a better cut has been aimed at. The standard colour, grey, has been maintained.

universal can. The large can or pail used by the kitchen staff to distribute tea, cocoa, or soup. Of approximately 2½ gallons capacity, one can supplies the needs of about 20 men. See *pail, food; diet tin; utensils*, etc.

unlock. The day watch comes on duty at about 6.15 a.m. The landing officers take up their positions, one to a landing, and each officer counts the occupied cells on his landing. The Orderly Officer or Principal Officer on duty then calls out the letter and number of each landing in turn. The officers answer with the number of men locked in; *e.g.* 'A.1.' calls the P.O., the officer in charge of 'A' Wing, No. 1 landing, then calls back the number of men he has counted. When all have thus been checked and the totals found correct the order is given, 'Unlock'. At once the officers race along the landings unlocking doors with an amazing dexterity. As each door is unlocked the cell occupant races out with his chamber pot and water jug. The first ones unlocked have the use of slop sink and tap; those who follow must queue up. The resultant stench at this hour is best left to the imagination.

Men due for discharge that morning are unlocked earlier with the kitchen hands and cleaners. See *landing; slop-out; open up*.

up the stairs. Assize Court. See *Follies*.

U.S. day. Fish day. This is the most unpopular meal of the week and is usually on a Friday. Sometimes fish is fried, for which fat from the cocoa is saved. Fried fish is popular and on occasions can be 'sold'. Usually fish is boiled and is served with cabbage and potato. Semolina pudding is usually given with this meal. 'U.S.' means 'Unconditional Surrender' and is a constant, overworked prison joke: the fish did not die, it made no struggle, but just surrendered unconditionally. See *diet*, etc.

Usk. Borstal Institution with accommodation for 213. Land is also farmed at Prescoed Camp by 'boys' from this establishment. See *Borstal Institutions*.

utensils (eating). Enamelled plates are used by all prisoners except Special Stage convicts. China mugs (one-pint size, referred to as P.P.'s) have replaced insanitary enamelled mugs. Knife, fork, and spoon are sometimes standard cell equipment, but where men eat in association the knives are collected after each meal. Washing up is done by the table orderlies and men who eat in cell must wash up as best they can at the slop sink. Food is served in diet tins, universal pails, and tin trays. See *diet tin; universal can*, etc., etc.

V

valuables. Small accessories such as gold or silver cuff-links, watches, studs, etc. These are kept, not in the *reception* (*q.v.*) with a man's *property* (*q.v.*), but in the Steward's Office. Money and documents are also kept by the Steward until the morning of a man's discharge.

van. 'The van' may refer to either the police flying-squad car or to the Black Maria or to the vehicle bringing up reinforcements to a police raid. See *heavy stuff; Sweeney; holler wagon; follow-up wagon*, etc.

V.C. Visiting Committee. A committee which pays periodical visits to prisons to hear complaints, to try those cases which are beyond the Governor's powers to adjudicate on, and to see that all is running smoothly. The Criminal Justice Act of 1948 calls for the Committee to have free access to every prison and to every man therein confined and such Committees to be comprised of J.P.'s, magistrates, etc., according to the direction of the Secretary of State. See *V.M.*

V.D. cells. In the big prisons a number of cells are reserved for men suffering from V.D. These men are not allowed beyond a defined limit and must use a separate recess, library, etc. See *itch pitch; isolation cells; scabies; T.B. library*, etc.

vice. Although Paris and Buenos Aires are so frequently regarded as cities of vice, London and possibly other big cities in this country can equal almost any other in the world for organised vice. Frequent reports of post-war years have shown the increases in prostitution, gaming, and drug-taking to be of alarming proportions. However, in the English prisons to-day there are few 'pimps and ponces'; those who are in prison are the small-time men. Drug addicts and drug dealers are rare and the number 'in' for gaming is infinitesimal.

Sexual vice exists in prisons, chiefly due to the fact that perverts and homosexuals are mixed in with the ordinary criminals. The chief danger here, where men have a certain amount of access to each other, is the corruption of young prisoners who, though sexually normal, will do anything or a great deal for payment in tobacco. The new Criminal Justice Act, with its broadened attitude towards the young offender, will do a great deal to suppress this existing evil. See *pimp; ponce; pouff; dope*, etc.

village, the. The villages belonging to the Prison Commission, where officers from the big convict prisons live. These big prisons have small villages adjoining, where only officers and their families live. Prisoners clean the streets and tend lawns and flower-beds, etc. See *gardens*.

villainy, to do a. To commit a burglary or other similar offence. Also, *perform; case; do*.

vine, the. The 'grapevine' or underground source of information. See *grapevine; buzz; tapped signals; quadratic alphabet; rumours*.

visits. A man is allowed one visit of half an hour's duration for every 28 days served. In the training centres this is increased to one every 21 days. A convict may save up a year's visits and move to a local prison nearer his home, where he may use them all up in a day or so. Visits can be forfeited by bad conduct or, by good behaviour, the Governor may grant an extension of time. Some men never have visits and, if they so wish, may have an extra letter for each visit due, but not *vice versa*.

Visits are held in small booths at the prison gate

(see *Zoo trip; closed visit*) or in a room under the supervision of an officer and separated by a table between prisoner and visitor (see *open visit*).

visits, legal and business. Extra visits may be granted, on application to the Governor, for visits from lawyers, their representatives, or persons holding power of attorney for a prisoner. See *power of attorney*.

visits, private. In a few prisons and under exceptional circumstances a trusted prisoner may be granted a private visit. He uses the glass-fronted room used for legal visits, where he can be seen but not overheard. All other visits are listened to by officers.

visits, sick. A man whose parent or wife or child is ill almost to the point of death may be given permission to visit such sick person. He travels in civilian clothes with one or more officers, also in civilian clothes, and should the journey necessitate a night away from his prison he must spend that night either in the nearest prison to his home or in a police cell.

V.M. Visiting magistrate. Each month a magistrate tours the prison workshops and dining-halls with a senior officer. Any prisoner with a legitimate complaint may put the details before the visiting magistrate. In each shop or hall the officer calls out, 'Any one for the visiting magistrate?' See *V.C.; petition*.

vocational training. At three prisons, Maidstone, Wakefield, and Wormwood Scrubs, there are whole-time vocational training courses. These run for about six months and men selected for them do no other work. They are in three subjects, Precision Engineering, Bricklaying, and Painting and Decorating. They are in charge of civilian instructors, and in the case of Engineering additional evening classes in maths are available. See *education*.

voltage. The lighting voltage in most prisons is stepped down to about 50 volts, as a precaution against would-be suicides. This lower voltage makes cigarette-lighting considerably easier for the man who has neither tinder, lighter, nor match in his cell. Cell lamps are of about 15 to 20 watts, but these have in many prisons been replaced by 40-watt lighting. In special cases some men studying may obtain permission to use a 60-watt lamp. This is very necessary where long hours of study are a great strain on a man's eyesight. See *lighting; suicide.*

W

Wakefield. Training centre with cell accommodation for 782. Although Wakefield was the original *training centre* (*q.v.*), it is now following the system employed at Maidstone (*q.v.*). New Hall Camp, attached to Wakefield, has accommodation for 100 men in huts. This was the forerunner of the *open-camp prison* (*q.v.*) and was instigated by Sir A. Paterson (*q.v.*), who also encouraged the formation of the Imperial Staff College (*q.v.*) for the training of new entries into the Prison Service.

Although statistics for comparison are not yet available for Maidstone, those for Wakefield show encouraging signs. Of *star* (*q.v.*) prisoners discharged from Wakefield from 1935 to 1942 inclusive, 87·8 per cent. had not been reconvicted of an offence by the end of 1944.

wall, the. The high wall, sometimes as high as 40 ft., surrounding the old fortress type of prison. These prisons are usually referred to as 'maximum security' prisons, and there will always be a need for such places, though, it is hoped, in decreasing numbers. The new prisons will not rely on walls to keep men in. That whitewashed boundaries are just as effective with some men has been proved at many new 'open-camp' (*q.v.*)

prisons. See *Ley Hill; Aldington Camp; New Hall Camp; Askham Grange,* etc.

A prisoner who manages to elude the vigilance of the officers and finally comes to the wall as his last obstacle is still not free. Without rope or ladder the average wall is unscaleable and only a man with exceptional 'commando' training could hope to clear it with rope alone. See *over the wall; have it away; escapee; escape list; wallflower; outfit.*

wall inspection. An officer tours the inside of the wall two or three times daily. Men frequently try to have packets of tobacco and/or money thrown over at a certain point, to be picked up by men working in the grounds. See *trafficking; snout,* etc.

wall party. Each year a party of men is put on to the job of repointing the wall of the prison. Those on the outside wall, working in the public road, have the advantage of being able to collect cigarette ends, which they re-roll to smoke or which they sell to men inside. See *outside parties,* etc.

wallflower. Escapee. One who talks of nothing else but (*a*) escaping, (*b*) 'how nice it will be when he gets outside'. Usually applied to the (*a*) class, who are convinced that one day they will make the perfect getaway. This type usually thinks no further than getting over the wall, which is comparatively easy when compared with the problem of *staying* away and avoiding detection and recapture during the succeeding years. See *have it away; outfit,* etc.

Wandsworth. London prison and Borstal with cell accommodation for 1,091. When a man at a training centre brags of coming from Wandsworth, it is known that he has previous convictions. See *Prisons,* etc.

war reserve. Officer who joined the service during the war, either voluntarily or through being 'directed' into it. These officers are looked down on by the regular prison officers, though many have since become regulars.

warders. In the Prison Service to-day warders are known as prison officers (*q.v.*) and the word warder is rarely heard in prison. See *screw; twirl; flue; bastard*, etc.

wash basins. Some of the more modern prisons have wash basins installed in the recesses and it is unnecessary for men to wash in cells. In some prisons the wash basins are for show only and it is a punishable offence to use them. See *ablutions; hot water; bath*, etc.

water pipes. The heating pipes which run through the cells in some prisons. Signals and messages can be, but rarely are, tapped on these. See *heating; tapped signals; quadratic alphabet*, etc.

wax. Black cobbler's wax, mixed in the mailbag shop for waxing thread before sewing. Wax is a popular amusement among men who spend a great deal of time locked in cell. It can be used for modelling, making dice, marbles, etc. See *mailbags; amusements; pastimes*.

waxing. Almost the first task given to a man entering prison. The waxing of thread for sewing mailbags is a monotonous and messy business. With a ball of wax in one hand the man pulls each strand of thread through it until it is properly waxed. This task is sometimes given to men who cannot be trusted with needle, scissors, or knife. See *mailbags; suicide*.

W.E.A. Workers' Educational Association. An organisation to encourage learning among working people and to promote understanding between all classes. The W.E.A. has many members who voluntarily take classes or give lectures in prisons. See *education*.

weaving. The weaving of scarves and table covers, etc., on small hand-looms is a popular hobby encouraged in such prisons as Maidstone (see *hobbies; education*). All cloth and other material for the making of prison clothing and bedding is woven at Wakefield. See *tailors*, etc.

week-end, a. Any short term of imprisonment. See *time; haircut.*

weighed off. Judged; sentenced. A Judge 'weighs off' the prisoner in the dock. The prison Governor 'weighs off' a prisoner guilty of some breach of regulations. See *do, to; done.*

welding. In the engineering shop or tinshop and often in the prison 'works' party, there is equipment for welding. This is a trade which a man can pick up in prison. See *education; vocational training.*

whank, to. To masturbate. See below.

whanker's doom. A man suspected of excessive masturbation is said to be suffering from 'whanker's doom'. See *gate fever; debtor's colic; prison rot; cobitis; convictitis.*

whisper. A rumour. Also, *buzz* (service).

white. Five pounds and upwards. Also, *crackle; handful; flim; red.*

white. Where jewellery is concerned 'white' is used to refer to platinum. See *snow; red; reddite; ice; jar.*

white. Silver; silver coins. See *silver; snow; pewter; arge; pony in white.*

white, pony in. Twenty-five shillings in silver. See above, etc.

white powder. The standard prison medicine, containing magnesia or peppermint, for any sort of stomach trouble. See *hospital*, etc.

Whitley Council. Official body which deals with conditions of service, etc., connected with members of the Prison Service.

whizz gang. A gang of pickpockets who work together. The 'whizz boys'. See *buzzing*.

whizzed. One who has been 'whizzed' is one who has had his pocket picked.

whizzer. A pickpocket. Also, *buzz; dip*.

whizzing. Pickpocketing in a gang.

'who dunnit?' (M). A meat pie. 'Who killed the prison cat?' 'There's a who-dunnit for dinner to-day.' See *meat pie; menu*, etc.

wide. 'Wise'; 'smart'.

wide boy. A 'smart alec'. Not easily caught. A 'spiv' is a 'wide boy', but a 'wide boy' is not necessarily a 'spiv' (*q.v.*). See *actor*.

Winchester. Local prison with accommodation for 395 men and a number of women. See *Prisons*.

windows. Windows in the old-type prisons are divided into about 28 small panes of glass. These panes are set in a heavy frame on the outside of which is a series of heavy bars built into the walls. Two small panes are movable and can be opened or closed at will (see *swinging a line*). It is an offence, according to the rules, to look out of a window. In any case it is necessary to stand on chair or table to reach the lowest panes, which are some six feet odd from the floor. See *T.B. cells*, etc.

women's prisons. Holloway and Aylesbury are the two principal women's prisons, in which are housed all categories of women prisoners and convicts, from Borstal girls to recidivists.

Local prisons with accommodation for women are:

Askham Grange	'open-camp' prison	Durham	105 cells
		Exeter	37 ,,
Birmingham	87 cells	Manchester	269 ,,
Cardiff	65 ,,		

Training centres have never been tried for women's prisons, except to a certain extent at Holloway. The Prison Commission expect to bring about radical changes in the whole treatment of women offenders. Mailbags are no longer made in women's prisons and the desire is that if sewing must be given them, it shall be constructive and directed more to the making of garments. One of the grimmest things of women's prisons has been the uniform. The large Victorian-servant type of apron, the shawl, and so on. These have already been done away with, to a certain extent, and the Commissioners have a Committee sitting on the important subject of women's dress, including underwear. The view is that women should be encouraged to take pride in their appearance and no longer forced to feel humiliated. Lipstick is allowed, but, as with pay and tobacco in men's prisons, the poor pay does not allow a woman much scope in this direction. Educational classes and training in domestic duties are encouraged among the younger women and expectant mothers are allowed to go to outside hospitals for confinement and to have their babies with them in prison. See *Prisons; Borstal Institutions.*

wood party. Party of men detailed to cut wood. Logs and kindling wood are cut for sale to the prison staff. Parties go out into the woods to fell trees; others cut waste wood from the carpenters' shop, or logs brought in by outside parties.

woodener. A man doing one month's imprisonment. In the 'old days' a prisoner was given a wooden spoon with which to eat. Also, at one time, the first part of a sentence was served without a mattress. The man slept on the wooden bed-board.

There is also a rhyming connection between three words connected with a month's sentence: 'woodener' —one who uses a wooden spoon—'moon', and 'spoon'. See also *time; moon.*

woodshed. The woodshed is generally in charge of a prisoner and when the weather does not permit outside parties such as the gardening party to work the men are employed chopping wood.

works party. The prison party which carries out repairs within the prison. Also called the *Engineer's Party*, because it comes under the direction of the prison Engineer. This is not to be confused with the Engineering *Course*, run as part of the *Vocational Training* (*q.v.*) Scheme. See also *'brickies'; builder's party; engineer.*

Wormwood Scrubs. Local prison for North London. Cell accommodation for 1,139 men. Accommodation in such prisons as this varies from time to time, according to current needs. The largest prison hospital is located here. See *Prisons; psychiatric unit.*

X

Xmas. See under *Christmas.*

X-rays. A number of prison hospitals are equipped with X-ray units. Where this facility is not available men needing such examination are sent out, under escort, to the nearest civilian hospital. See *hospital; escort.*

Y

Yanking. Popular expression to describe the activities of girls who specialise in picking up American soldiers.

Yard, the. Scotland Yard.

yard lavatories. Any outside lavatory.

yard redband. The redband (*q.v.*) detailed to keep all yards and lavatories clean and tidy (see *karzy cleaner*). He is sometimes in charge of the incinerator, where he disposes of all sweepings, etc.

yards, the. The exercise grounds and spaces about the prison enclosure. The exercise yards are usually three cement paths round which men walk in circles (see *exercise*). Lavatories are situated on all exercise yards and men are encouraged to use them during exercise time. The difficulty starts when, in winter, all outside lavatories are frozen up, and their condition is best imagined.

Y.C. Young convict. Men under twenty-one years of age are lodged apart from the older men. They are accorded certain privileges, such as extra bread and potatoes. They are given compulsory P.T. at least once a day, where there is a qualified officer available. During the daytime they mix with the others in the workshops and yards. They are referred to as 'the Y.C.'s' and, in local prisons, as 'Y.P.'s' or 'young prisoners'.

Under the new *Criminal Justice Act*, 1948 (*q.v.*), no man under twenty-one years of age shall be sent to prison unless 'the court is of the opinion that no other method of dealing with him is appropriate' (Ch. 58, p. 1. 17, Criminal Justice Act, 1948).

In place of imprisonment there will be detention

centres where offenders between the ages of fourteen and twenty-one will be sent.

yellow peril. Carrot soup (also called 'loop the loop', in rhyming slang). This is a frequent item on the prison menu, generally on Thursdays, when there is only a pint of this soup, sometimes a few potatoes, and a 'duff'. See *diet; menu; duff*.

young tart. Any young girl; any 'teen-ager'. See *tart*.

Y.P. Young prisoner. See *imp; P.S.; Criminal Justice Act*, 1948.

Z

zombie. Any particularly 'miserable' officer may be referred to as a 'zombie'. One who gives the impression of being more dead than alive.

Zoo trip. A 'box' visit. The dismal little booth with glass and wire screen which separate the prisoner from his visitor. See *visits; closed visit*.

For Product Safety Concerns and Information please contact our EU
representative GPSR@taylorandfrancis.com
Taylor & Francis Verlag GmbH, Kaufingerstraße 24, 80331 München, Germany